MOUNTAINS AND VALLEYS

Poetry-An Evolution of Belief

Philip Carmen

Amazon

ISBN-13: 9798351751856
ISBN-10: 1477123456

Cover design by: Art Painter
Library of Congress Control Number: 2018675309
Printed in the United States of America

Dedicated to my wonderful wife Shirley who truly lives her Christian life and has made my life better than I would have ever dreamed.

CONTENTS

INTRODUCTION

"For God so loved the world that he gave his one and only Son, that whoever believes in him shall not perish but have eternal life" John 3v16

At the age of twenty I realized my life had little purpose and meaning. Emotionally I was becoming unstable. What I needed was an anchor for my soul. A friend brought me to faith in the Lord Jesus Christ and I felt renewed in mind, body and spirit. I was born again. No longer was I wandering aimlessly like the rat in the poem I wrote but had found purpose to my existence. But as time went by, I realized that Christianity was not an easy path. Mathew 7v 13-14 says "Enter by the narrow gate. For the gate is wide and the way is easy that leads to destruction, and those who enter by it are many. For the gate is narrow and the way is hard that leads to life, and those who find it are few"

The wonderful thing about life is that as you grow older your life changes. What you believed over forty years ago you come to realise things in an entirely different way, no longer are you so dogmatic about things as you were when young. So, these poems were formed in my earlier days when I felt things more deeply, but now I drift along in the flow and accept these poetic verses as a stage in my development as a human being. As poems I do so hope they inspire from purely an artistic as well as an encouraging way. I suppose, if I were honest, I would admit to believing in a personal god but not a god controlled by established church practices. In that way I feel a kindred spirit to all creatures on this beautiful Earth. There is so much beauty in the bible but not all the bible is meant to be taken literally. Some of it is creation myth and other parts are allegorical yet essentially there is deep truth. Yet for those not blessed with faith the words of moral guidance remain applicable whatever stage you are in your life and beautiful in an aesthetically pleasing way.

As human-beings I believe we evolved and so believe that what we believe in evolves as well. Truth is not just confined to Christian thoughts. Truth can be found in philosophy, sociology, scientific speculation and all the belief systems past and present but especially in the world of poetry because you are dealing with not only conscious thought but the subconscious where dwells an endless source of knowledge about the world we live in and our emotional attachment to it.

Along with the highs of the ecstasy of belief

and faith there are the trials of Christian in The Pilgrims Progress who travelled through the Valley of the Shadow of Death. In fact, we learn more about ourselves and God in the valleys (our low times) than we ever do on the high mountains (our high times). Suffering teaches us to depend upon God. For those who believe He is the source of our life and he walks with us through life's travails. So, these poetry insights are my coping mechanism to help me on my journey and I hope they help you, my friends. PJC

MOUNTAINS AND VALLEYS
(To Be a Christian)

Thus says the Lord, because the Syrians have said 'The Lord is God of the hills but is not God of the valleys, therefore I will give all this great multitude into your hand, and you shall know that I am the Lord'. 1Kings 20v28

"I know not how I seem to others, but to myself I am a small child wandering upon the vast shores of knowledge, every now and then finding a small bright pebble to content myself with while the vast ocean of undiscovered truth lay before me." Sir Isaac Newton

Commitment

As I walk with you
our needs are met,
the road less rugged;
no need to fret.

As I talk with you
all self-thoughts flee.
My eyes fresh set
on only Thee.

THE RAT

A little rat
upon river bank bare
hunted for food
which wasn't there.
Its nose twitched
this way and that
in incessant searching
till at last it sat,
to look around at the world
so profound
and study its secrets
if it could;
but unable to
it scurried around
for it knew it never would.

While at work on a plant nursery I saw this rat
wandering aimlessly about and it struck me that
I was a bit like that; aimless and unfocussed. I
needed a sense of purpose to my life. A reason to
be.

BELIEF

Sometimes I believe I can fly
yet my splintered body makes me cry;
especially now laying on this bed of straw
I believe I need that faith even more
so, I can spread my wings above the hurt of
earth;
accept my lot in soul's rebirth.

Sometimes a fog appears to take away my sight
and I drift appallingly into night
hating this body for all its worth;
its then I need a soul's rebirth
to stop the lies that blind me to all that's good,
stop me forever thinking of that awful word
'should!'

Should have been made stronger now,
should have got my head to bow,
should have accepted long ago
that 'should' and 'would' stops the rivers flow,
the river of life that run through me to the rest
of humanity.

Just help me Lord to remember to smile
as I rest my body for a while.
Remember to not lose sight of hope
that helps me float my little boat
out in the rough and hurtful sea
that I share with the rest of humanity.

I must fly and I must float
above the hurts that attempt to sink my boat.
I must soar above the storm
where the sun is shining bright and warm
and even with this fragile body I possess

I have Gods love and know his sweet caress.

A YOUNG BOY SITS

Upon a rock a young boy sits,
Staring out to sea.
In front of him lies his future years;
Behind lays history.

And as if one thought were not enough
Another thought appears
And he wonders what the future holds;
How long he has in years.

But as he watches, the tide comes in.
Inexorably, times sand disappears;
behind, evening shadows increase,
With them comes a sombre peace
That as a blanket covers him.

'Now hope that is seen is not hope. For who hopes
for what he sees? But if we hope for what we do
not see, we wait for it with patience' Romans
8v24, 25

WALK IN THE LIGHT
(masks)

Sometimes Lord, even now I believe I wear a mask.
A mask is a front hiding something different
beneath.
Even now I must seem to people that which I am
not.
More than ever this mask, that is not me, must be
stripped off to reveal that which lies beneath the
surface.

Maybe this mask hides deep regret, fear or
inferiority?
The mask smiling yet the eyes through the holes
telling the truth of that which lies in the heart.

Please tell me if I am not being the real me.
Please speak the truth! I know it will hurt,
but no honest revelation can possibly come
without hurt.
No one that is brought into the light of truth can
be quite the same.

Be truthful to me. With your truthfulness my
salvation depends.
With your love, the real me, you being a major part
is given more room to grow.

YOU

Am I really real?

What does reality mean to some one
like me adrift between love and a dream?
Reality to someone like me is more
than being able to see, touch or smell.

Yet, what is reality to someone like you
who knows me so well?

The one thing I know is that I love you so.
To touch you sets my heart aglow;
and the scent of you is more fragrant by far
than all of the flowers in the world.

And when you are not with me
to know you is enough.
That will have to suffice for now.

STRUGGLE OR SWIM WITH ME?

I sat by the seashore and thought,
'How could people swim in such a sea?'
The waves are as big as a house.
The current stronger beneath than above,
and my heart in doubt troubles me.
Then I said to my Lord,
'How can this be?'
How can I combat this doubt in me?"
Then he said, 'By love and faith in me.'

So, I took his hand and he walked with me
to the edge of the sounding sea.
I heard him say, 'Struggle or swim with me?'

So, I took his word as courage, dived on in,
not knowing or caring if I would rise again.
But we arose together, my Lord and me
and now we swim forever in the sounding sea.

MORE THAN CONQUEROR

You are all heart.
Your love soothes me,
caresses me
and I am well again.

Love in the form of tears
combine to remove my fears.

Love in the form of words
command a blessing.

Love raids my fortress home;
tearing out the bars from the windows,
the unyielding oaken door,
so, gaining entrance
to my enslaved heart;
making your home there.

NO CONDEMNATION

When I have seen thee
heavy tread
the path
that sought
to condemn
a man
for being wrong,
so, lose a friend.

I would rather
take upon me
all his blame
and meekly tread
the path he trod
for even so
it led to God
and left its
scars and pain
on Calvary.

THE HILLSIDE

When I was young the hillside was my place of
peace,
the gentle walk beneath gathered pines,
the woodland floor littered with needles and
cones.
I had to reach the lush grassland, stopping awhile
upon the summit and just while an hour or two
away;
thanking God and talking to Him.

Now that I have grown, the passage of time
compressed into barely enough breathing space,
I reminisce about the carefree days
when I communed with God alone.

Yet in my heart I now see clearly
as I pass through the mists into God's sensitivity.
Into His Presence that is nearer by far than the
hillside of my youth,
the constant need for quietness.

Now in the bustle of everyday activity,
the responsibility of life's calls on every side,
my quietness must dwell within
my heart becoming God's hillside.

LIGHT

"Who stands at the door and knocks?"

I am the man who has come to an end:
an end of all struggle and strife,
high ideals, ambition and planning.
There is so much that I have not experienced of
life,
so much that I do not know; only the reality
that you open the door when someone knocks,
and the certainty that it is right to do so.

When I opened the door to you, Lord
I was a vessel emptied of the knowledge that I
knew the way.
Lost as I was in my sin, I was lost for the words to
say,
lost to a world bent on destruction and vice
having broken all promises, set in its lies.

I opened the door to let the light in.
It revealed me in poverty, locked in my sin.
You unlocked my door, releasing your love to heal
me within.
Now I am unburdened, unashamed and in need of
loving.

'The Lord is God, and he has given us light' Psalm
118v27

IN GOD ALONE

A ship at anchor is my soul,
not moving out to sea
but resting in my father's arms
until He sends me.

Until He sends me forth
into a vast and unfathomable ocean
where the waves are high,
the water deep;
where I must trust in Him alone.

"And we know that God causes everything to work
together for the good of those who love God and
are called according to his purpose for them."
Romans 8v28 NLT

THE ROCK

Lord, let not my every word be bitter,
tinged with deep regret.
The spring flows forth from my heart.
Lord, clean up the bitter spring.
You have suffered enough.
Instead of selfishness
let there be worshiping.
Let worship flood my soul.
Lord, break the dam of selfishness within.
Let me bring thankfulness as my offering.
Let me not manipulate with every heart-rending
word.
The mud oozing from the wound like treacle
makes an everglade of misery.

Am I not part of the Rock?
That sacrificed His life that I might live?
Jesus my one delight,
change the course of Your River
that flows from my heart.
Make it a place of peace and not remorse.
A place of love and not divorce.
A haven of rest and not restlessness.
A poultice of healing upon the hurt of man.

"Hearken to me, you who pursue deliverance,
you who seek the Lord; look to the rock
from which you were hewn, and to the quarry

from which you were digged "Isaiah 51v1

"The Lord is my rock. And my fortress, and my deliverer; My God, the strength, in whom I will trust; my buckler, and the horn of my salvation, and my high tower." Psalm 18v2

Poetry has helped me to overcome 30 years of chronic pain and a degenerative spinal injury and the disibility it causes every day to my body, and often to my mind.. Having a faith has also taken the burden off my bodily condition and the stress it causes. Beauty that I find in nature, and words that express that beauty, I applaud with all my heart. I can truthfully say that I love my life and all the people who have stood by me in my darkest times. Love is light and light will always overcome the darkness.

TOUCH ME

We have hope, whose hearts are open wide,
having shared ourselves and often cried.
There is no love where there is no meeting.
Lives which speak at a distance
bring little comfort.
You need to touch to
appreciate the sores and cuts;
the hurts others feel.
You need to hold to bring relief
from pain and fear;
only tenderness restores.
When we are distant
we cannot feel the hurt others feel.
We need to hold and find each other.
Risk the pain of separation,
anger and the desperate cry for help
that surfaces when love is shared,
grief awakened.
You touch me and hold me tight
and I will live to be alright.
Reach out to me and hold my hand
and we will walk into the Land.

PATIENCE

Who knows what the future holds!
God does
and he bestows
patience
as the fertile soil
to protect the seed
he sows.

"But if we hope for what we do not see, we wait for
it with patience" Romans 8v25

RESURRECTION

There seems no shadow anymore.
They have dispersed
like so many times before
when the sun has risen
and challenged their domain.
No longer will they come again.

Only if allowed to come
out of a weakness yet undefined,
encroaching on my life like a noise.
Dissipating harmony,
creating discord;
not a song.

Yet the sun has come
and with its life and heat
harmony is restored.
There is left now only a sense of peace.

PILGRIMS WAY

He walks the Pilgrims Way one more time
towards the city of Canterbury,
as the faithful from many lands
congregate in the holy sanctuary.

The man in the street cannot understand
that the pilgrim travels for God not man.
He has chosen a solitary path
and carries a burden hard to bear.
He is glad to hear cathedral bells
calling the faithful to prayer.

THE ROAD TO EMMAUS

Troubled, not only by the incessant heat,
the long and dusty road to Emmaus.
Troubled so that we could hardly dare to speak,
yet we had to, desperately needed to speak.
Troubled by doubt, disappointed and feeling so
alone.
With so many questions but so few answers:
only rumours, unbelievable rumours
but we so wanted to believe them.
Who is the stranger that walks with us?
He certainly has the bearing of a sage.
Certainly, he is friendly enough, and so wise.
What questions he asks, and what answers he
gives!
Somehow, he may have the answers that we
need.
Somehow, we have to keep him by our side.
Somehow, we recognize in him someone,
maybe
who we once knew so very well,
but who now seems so distant, so very distant,
out of reach and out of sight, just out of mind.
It is only as he stops with us to eat.
Only as he breaks the bread do we see his
hands,
look down at his feet;
see wounds still visible and deep;

see eyes compassionate and meek.
Our hearts are melted with the heat of
recognition.

Master, Master, we kneel down at your feet!

"Their eyes were opened, and they recognised
him"

Luke 24v31

No man is an Island

No man is an island entire of itself; every man
is a piece of the continent, a part of the main;
if clod be washed away by the sea, Europe
is the less, as well as if a promontory were, as
well as any manner of thy friends or of thine
own were; any man's death diminishes me,
because I am involved in mankind.
And therefore never send to know for whom
The bell tolls; it tolls for thee. John Donne

FOUR WEEKS OLD

Four weeks old,
only a spec in the vastness of eternity,
small as small can be, yet every moment
growing larger,
every moment developing
her own unique print
upon the human race.
Her own special personality
enriching this globe,

And I am stunned
that so much potential is
wrapped in so fragile a frame.
So much love that in the future
will burst forth from her
like a mighty river-

Flooding this world with her Jesus song.

BRAYFORD WHARF

Through Brayford Wharf the river runs
serene and fast beneath a springtime sun.
Of Lincoln Cathedral, a shadow cast
that creates a sense of age, so vast.

On every street corner you can see
the interminable steps of history.
On Easter Sunday pilgrims pray
and darkness is dispersed for another day.

At Brayford Wharf the students spend
fruitful times chatting and drinking wine.
They share camaraderie as special in its way
as the loyal pilgrims that kneel and pray.

I watch the swans as they glide
and feel a renewed sense of pride
knowing that life goes on, as it must
until all of life returns to dust.

Far above the water church bells sound out for
prayer.
Of nature's tranquil song I am well aware.
Students sit in bars: their cathedral stall,
knowing deep down inside, one day, this world
must fall.

Yet while friendships grow, as grow they must
love will arise like a phoenix from the dust.
Nature casts its enchantment far and wide

and from its spell no-one can hide.

I am spellbound by the waters flow
and feel a peace inside me grow.
Cathedral bells are ringing now
and I see life written on a flower.

Life is written for all to see
and stored within our memory.
We are made richer not by what we own
but by how much care is shown.

At Brayford Wharf two students
hug each other tight.
In Lincoln Cathedral prayers
are prayed this very night.

FREEDOM

I escaped from my prison cell
for years it's been a living hell
and I've been quite unwell.

This year the bars dissolved in front of me,
my exile is now a part of history.
The crippling illness that kept me trapped
within,
that harboured me inside jetty walls of sin.

My craft broke free from its moorings.
I am free to make for open sea.
My exile is now part of history.

Now free to voyage in seas of mystery
where there are no boundaries for my soul,
now that poetry and faith has made me
whole,
and I am travelling on the wind of prayer.

Ages ago the enemy as a siren calling me
to wreck upon the rocks of my instability.
One day past he caught me unaware;
I let my guard down and he kept me bound
to my self-pity and suffering.

Today I saw the sun rise on my horizon.

Some dolphins follow my crafts wake
making me feel rejuvenated and set free,
shaking the hurt and suffering from off me,
setting others like me free, for Jesus sake.

"I Am Your Peace"

Make peace with me.
A storm arose within your heart
when someone spoke ill of you,
swirling around like angry clouds
your restless emotions
thundered and were proud.

"I speak to you; be still you troubling winds!"
 "Be calm you troubled sea,
   if you would my servant be!"
 For I desire a better you,
only asking that you desire
more of me."

"For, now in Christ Jesus you who once were far off
have
  been brought near in the blood of Christ.
  For He is our peace." Ephesians 2v13

GOD INCREASES

How does the river know
where it must flow?
Once it has sprung
from the earth as a spring,
or from mountain top heights,
begun its downward flowing,
into the valley and then to the sea,
following the line of least resistance;
flowing around obstacles
that stands in its way.
It bends and it twists
and it broadens while on its way,
catching more water on its journey
to the sea.
So, I like a river
flows on to the sea
taking the course of least resistance,
bending and twisting my ways
to suit Thee.
Widening and deepening
my response to Your Will,
allowing Your Spirit to fill me until
I overflow the banks,
pouring blessing beside
the dry and needy soil
where hurt ones abide.
I follow the course set before me

by God who has power
and desires to bring release
  by His blood in this hour.
    Who knows where the river will flow?
    Onward, I trust, till His purpose I know,
    fully revealed in His Almighty Son.
All that I need to is obediently flow,
knowing His purpose is being done.
If I myself decrease
  and let Him increase and grow,
    lost in His Immensity, seaward I flow.

A CHILD

We are much too complicated
living this life must be simpler
than we make it to be.
We need to be as a child
sitting on our father's knee.

Silence

Silence is but a short respite
before the clang of cymbals
the staccato of voices rat-a-tatting:
filling the void with some noisy form.

I prefer to leave things be.
To let my silence, speak for itself.
To not get bogged down in having to say anything.
To appreciate silence when it comes
like a balm to take the aches away.
For without silence there can be no renewal.

Everyone needs the silent place within their soul.

I often seek the silence of tranquillity-
Only there can my spirit be set free.

LOVE

A ray of sunlight has come to make a visit.
He let himself in through
the window of my eyes
and set himself down
upon a seat provided-

That happened to be my heart.

"But for you who obey me, my saving power
will rise on you like the sun and bring healing like
the sun's rays" Malachi 4v2

PATIENCE

Who knows what the future holds!
God does
and he bestows
patience
as the fertile soil
to protect the seed
he sows.

"But if we hope for what we do not see, we wait for
it with patience" Romans 8v25

GODS LIKENESS

A portrait in repose?
No: lifelike and it flows
through life's landscape:
So vast, and yet it grows.

The possibilities are endless.
Each interaction limitless.
It has the mark of genius
that only an artist knows.

I and you are Gods creation.
Each one unique, yet incomplete
until painted alongside one another;
where hands and hearts can reach.

And with Gods limitless supply of grace,
His inestimable love,
I rise, an infinite being;
stretched beyond myself;
receiving Gods providential wealth:

Seeing myself as He sees me.

JOY COMES IN THE MORNING

I wept-

My pillow drenched with tears
as I emptied my heart of grief and fears.
The night clung to my turgid soul
like a rabid dog and would not let me go.

It seemed an age when first I put myself to bed;
an age when the walls and ceiling crowded in.
Time had stopped or I felt it had stopped.
My bedside clock stopped ticking
and I felt so very alone.

No-one felt the burden I was feeling.
No-one bore the pain I was bearing.
No-one understood my despairing.
Then day breaks out through corridors of dark
where creatures lurk in corners
and with the light creatures depart
as if the keeper of the dark is calling.

Lord, my heart feels no more the agonies of night.
Nor the hurt and fight, now Lord that your light is
falling.
Now Lord that joy fills up the gap,
hours before were full of black and in tears I called
your name;
felt the first slow ebbing of the pain;
knew then that you had heard, were near

and I was safe within your keeping-

Now I am gently sleeping.

Amazing Love by Charles Wesley

Amazing Love! How can it be
that Thou, my God, should'st die for me?

No condemnation now I dread;
Jesus, and all in Him is mine;
alive in Him, my living Head,
and clothed in righteousness divine,
bold I approach the eternal throne,
and claim the crown, through Christ my own

DAISY

Daisy in the grass
you make me smile.
Daisy in the sunshine
I look at you awhile

I know you are only small
as am I, little flower,
yet small things can
possess amazing power
to please the heart
and calm the mind.

Little things as you and I
are not so bothered by the fly
that would rather hover over sweet scented rose
than alight upon a small one's cloths.
Such simple textures, colours yellow and white.
you spread your petals in the sunlight.

So happy do you make me feel
as I upon the grass do kneel,
looking into your lovely face,
seeing more clearly

Gods wondrous grace.

THE JOY OF THE LORD

Sadness was the consuming pain,
grief the heavy mantel hard to bear
settled on my weary frame, then your word,
dear Jesus came, 'Accept my joy, even amidst this
pain.'

Accept I did His joy to me,
a stream of living water flowed.
It was His joy that set me free;
I almost laughed, the love He showed.

It settled on my weary frame.
He took away my mortal pain.
The grief inside me was relieved.
Joy filling my soul wherein I grieved.

'to give them a garland instead of ashes, the oil
of gladness Instead of mourning, the mantle of
praise instead of faint spirit' Isaiah 61v3

GROWTH OUT OF HARDSHIP

Out of the ash heap
grows a rose.
Out of the waste ground
a life exposed.
Exposed to the elements;
alien ground.
Dirt and dismal
yet new life abounds.
Thriving in hardship;
growing more each day,
raising its branches
joyfully.

'For he grew up before him like a young plant,
And like a root out of dry ground' Isaiah 53v2
'he lifts the needy from the ash heap, to make
them sit with princes 1 Samuel 2v7

TAKEN CAPTIVE TO CHRIST

He takes my life
and puts to flight
the wild enchantment
of the night.

He takes my heart
and with its heat
disperses evil
and the company it keeps.

He takes my words
and makes them His,
using them
to bring His peace.

He takes my thoughts,
transcending pain
and writes on them
His Holy name.

Lips that kiss.
Heart that feels.
Words that speak.
Thoughts that kneel.

SOUL

They are fading now,
the memories.
The hurt I felt
seems now so distant.
Memories only hurt
if you let them.
The good times-
And there were good times
seem more important now somehow
than they did then.
Better to remember
the sweetest scent,
the richest, most fragrant bloom
than see the petals discolour
and fade too soon.
The times I have lived through
have helped me to grow.
The winter winds still bring the snow
but I look forward to the Spring.
As a river, my life will always flow
onward till I reach the sea,
and find the most important part of me
lives onward to eternity.

THE POTTER

He holds this clay,
It is all I am-
a piece of clay in the Potter's hands.
Here in this life but a span.
He breaths His life into me and I am.

Upon His wheel He spins me round.
Moulds and breaks the hardness out.
I become suppler in His hands
and do His will as I should do.

"What right has the clay to tell the Potter what to
do?"
I shout, "Please do it quickly, Lord."
And he speaks "What I need to do I do."

"Why Lord am I so stubborn that you need
to break me as you do?"
He says, "My love is gentle, pure and kind;
my spirit requires a humbler you."

Self in Your hands, I am undone,
am broken, Lord, let Your will be done,
that you may mould me with the self-same clay
into Your Beloved Son.

PUZZLE

I know so little,
but think I know so much.
So much has been written,
yet so little is known.
Our universe is
one big puzzle.
I don't know how
to unravel the puzzle.
Only the one who
created
the puzzle
knows.

EVEN IN THE VALLEY
(guardian angel)

As I walked through this valley of fear,
the sun hidden, no one near
enough to lend a hand
or maybe even understand.
Above my head, the overhanging cliff
encroached upon my mood.
Sombre memories diffused
into a somewhat morbid frame
that had a form, and once a name.
    My heart was heavy.
    Your memory is all I had left of you.
    An unbearable hurt, too fresh to share
    left me wondering "Did no-one care?"
And as I walked, head sunk low,
I spied a flower that had surprising power
even in this valley, to grow.
    Its petals were so soft to touch,
    with powerful fragrance I loved so much
    that tears began to flow.
    Healing seeped into this tired old soul
    that was fast becoming whole.

What other wonders can I see
within this dark and lonely valley.
Maybe someone cares after all.
Maybe someone prays for me.

I see sunlight glistening in a pool.
See my reflection, and another
stands beside of me.
    He desires me to know that he
    will always be by my side,
    and cares enough no more to hide.
 He whispers in my ear,
    "I understand: I know!"

"For he will order his angels to protect you in all
you do." Psalm 91v11

HIDDEN

Hidden in the arms of love
self is unseen
when love is truly love.

No hand knows
what the other hand gives
when love is truly love,
the time when Jesus truly is
and I am hidden in Him,
and I am never seen;
clothed in His righteousness.

That is the time when I am less.
The time when He is more,
to know what I am living for;
to glorify Him who gives
me life and breath;
learning from Him how to love and bless.

To yield completely and be lost
in His tender loving kindness.

"Your life is hid with Christ in God" Colossians 3v3

FAITHFULNESS

A friend I knew was faithful.
In times of stress, he held my hand.
He rejoiced and wept with me at will
and in many battles, we fought together side by side.
Many victories, many disappointments, many failures
but he took the other oar and we rowed in stroke.
My life I owe to such loyalty.
God endows more to those who endure together.
He honours best those who share the most.

'I thank God whom I serve with a clear conscience
as did my fathers, when I remember you
constantly in my prayer. As I remember your tears,
I long night and day to see you, that I may be filled
with joy' 2 Timothy 1v3,4

ALL THAT'S LEFT

Am cursed to tread the path I tread
in this shadow world of living dread
with pools of acid and sulphur smell;
I shudder in the bowels of hell.

There is no end in mortal sight,
am much too petrified to fight,
am left immobile by my fear.
Is there no other person near
to share my inevitable fate?

Am I paying for my stupid pride and hate?
I long for woman's soft caress.
Every day I lose myself, becoming less.
In my path lies a molten river flowing.
My torment is forever growing.

I see hope only fleetingly now.
No longer has it might or power
to open heavens window wide
and quell this cruel tormenting tide.

My eyes have flinched from too much pain.
Must hide this hurt within my brain.
Must lose myself in fantasy
else die in my fragile humanity.

More shadows encroach upon me now.
They hold me within their hideous power.

Must repent, else lose my soul and mind
as have unnumbered souls of my kind.

I run as the fox from harm way.
The hounds of hell behind me bay:

All that's left to do is pray.

BRIDGES

Bridges of trust how they need to span culture,
race and clan.
Open hearts need open hands.
There is no going back once that gulf is crossed;
know where to go back to for you were alone and
lost.

The only difference between us is how far we have
come.
I have crossed over to your side.
All I ask is that you respond.
Respond to my act of friendship.
Love always seems to die more than it lives
yet it is so blessed to give;
to cross over and win your hand;

water of distrust transformed into fertile land.

NO, NOT UNFAIR

A cloud has dimmed the sun
but I'm not that far away.
Closer than feet and hands,
hear you when you pray.

Only a cloud of pity lays between us.
A layer of 'doesn't anybody care.'
You have all you need when you have me.
Don't expect life to always be fair.

It wasn't fair to go through all I did
that you might receive my love
but I didn't see it as unfair knowing
as I did my Fathers love from Heaven above.

Setting you free was my greatest joy
and I didn't regret that cost.
Freedom for all mankind the prize:
Saving the sheep that was lost.

'By this we know love, that he laid down his life for
us;
 and we ought to lay down our lives for the
brethren' 1John 3v16

THE TOTAL SUM

Sum it up, how much does that come to?
Weighed in a balance it weighs very little
but it is not the quantity that counts, only the quality.

Like my life. Weighed in a balance it doesn't amount to much but I hope the quality bears inspection.
Love is the only element that will have lasting value.
Love bears the royal seal of approval.

If I love then I am fulfilling my true obligation to the human race,
counting it a privilege to be on the receiving end
of someone else's love, at least once in a while.

'Listen to me, O house of Jacob, all you who remain of the house of Israel, you whom I have upheld since you were conceived, and have carried since your birth. Even to your old age and grey hairs. I am he, I am he who will sustain you. I have made you and I will carry you; I will sustain you and I will rescue you' Isaiah 46v3,4

WILDERNESS

What love I had has gone, wandered into some
desert place;
a wilderness of grace where no pools of water are.
Heartbroken, I seek hope for my soul, where I can
again
be whole and look out from a high place
yet I know there is a stream of water flowing
endlessly:

A place to drink until I'm full; a flowing stream; a
refuge of liberty.

Love returns from its wanderings in the
wilderness.
Love seeks and finds a place of rest, a sanctuary
within my breast;
there, Jesus, you made your home-

No longer need I roam.

'My Lord is near to the broken hearted, and saves
the crushed in spirit Psalm 34v18

SORROW NO MORE

Wake up my soul!
Let us leave this pain behind
and see what we can find
beyond the sorrow that we bear.

With a little care we may find
a friend who is so warm and kind.
A friend who wipes away our tears;
who will protect us from our fears.

Lord, will I find such a friend?
Who will never shun me or pretend.
Who will instead share his loaf of bread;
release my spirit from this dread.

My son, within you is an endless spring
that once release new life will bring.
Fresh hope for all humanity
as living water journeys to the sea.

God loves you more than life you know.
He made the seed from which you grow.
He made the earth, the sky and sea.
He spoke a word and let it be-

He lives in you and he lives in me.

EDEN

Sad is my eyes, my heart, my head.
I'm sad in every way that my life's been led.
Sadness consumes me in every part;
an axe has sliced my poor old heart.

An axe of doubt has sought to harm
my innocence and sense of calm.
Wild brambles are choking my peace of mind,
my sense of worth cannot unwind.

Bindweed smothers blooms that grow;
my heart has no room to flower you know.
My garden rest is overgrown.
The dove of peace has nearly gone,

Flown away upon a wind of care
where there is no sign that says 'Beware!'
'Beware of faded dreams that will not grow;
they cannot breathe amongst the hedgerow.

The Gardener comes and sees my state of mind.
He eradicates weeds of every kind,
leaving a sanctuary of bliss
that I had really come to miss.

Free now to find myself again
without this sense of all my shame
that hindered me in times of thought;
causing my cluttered life to abort.

God is my Gardener and in Him I find my rest.
In Eden, my heart is truly blessed.

A FOUNTAIN

Do I desire the things you desire, my Lord?
Am I serious enough to want what you want to
happen?
Or am I an armchair to sit in, a cup of tea in my
hand
and a smug smile upon my face?
Satisfied at how life is passing me by.
The clock does not stop for me.
Time passes and this moment in time will not
occur ever again.
The present all the time being replaced by the
future.
Each moment is important to you, Lord,
for, now is the day of salvation and each day
can be a fresh opportunity missed of showing
your love
or a fountain of life for those who seek life.

Make me a fountain and not a sponge.
A two-way pipe where your Spirit can flow
continually
and not a swamp where all streams emerge only to
stagnate and evaporate.
Lord, please make me an instrument of your
peace,
a song whose melody brings release.

"For with thee is the fountain of life; in thy light do

we see light" Psalm 36v9

IN THE STEPS OF THE MASTER

Do we really know what it's like to tread the path
that Jesus trod,
or taste the dirt of constant hurt, as well as the
grapes of love?
To climb to the top of every mountain peak; know
victory with every prayer.
But do we know the valley depths of hurt and deep
despair?

For I have walked them both before. I follow after
my Masters call;
know His glorious presence in answered prayer;
known Him to pick me up when I did fall.

'Fear not, I will help you' Isaiah 41v13
'my help comes from the Lord, who made heaven
and earth. He will not let your foot be moved'
Psalm 121v2,3

MAKE YOUR MARK

Knowing Your nearness
my heart is overthrown.
Knowing your nearness
my heart is a poem

created from such tender thought,
put together with sacrificial grace,
grafted into a living word;
making its mark upon the human race.

"Because he cleaves to me in love, I will deliver
him;
   I will protect him, because he knows my name.
When he calls to me, I will answer him; I will be
with him in trouble, I will rescue him and honour
him. With long life I will satisfy him and show
him my salvation.'
Psalm 91v14-16

HIS CHILD

I'm His child
I need not hide.
Am hid in Him,
my sins are covered.

He is my king,
I'm subject to Him,
all that I need He supplies-

Am encourage, never smothered.

'Beloved, we are Gods children now' 1 John 3v2

FAN THE FLAMES

When I was young
the fire was bright,
my zeal was fierce;
my heart was light.

Now as I've grown
my fires have grown dim.
Burdens of life
have quenched my flame.

A friend has come
and fanned my flame;
brought me to life
in Jesus name.

He came,
an encouraging glow
to rekindle faith
and help me grow.

To give me hope
and help me live
that I myself
can help and give.

'A friend loves at all times' Proverbs 17v17

THE RACE

I see with different eyes now,
things before I did not see.
The hedgerow blooms with new life now.
There is so much wonder in a tree.

Birds, they sing a freedom song
and I am left in awe
that so much that is good in life
is so completely ignored.

Self, consume our every thought.
We seldom ponder at God's Grace.
We wander through life like refugees
while others run the race.

'Do you not know that in a race all the runners
compete, but only one receives the prize? So run
that you may obtain it! 1 Corinthians 9v24

KNEE HIGH

Only knee high- Yet know the need to be loved.
Too small for much intellectual thought
yet needs a firm embrace.
Depending upon another human being.
Depends upon God
for all things.
Same as me,
over knee high
yet needing someone
higher than I.
Someone who can meet
my need for loving.
Someone who can give a firm embrace;
who can lead me in life's race;
can encourage and commend.
Who can say "I am your friend."
I was higher still yet I came down
and dwelt among your kind
as a man so, I could understand.
And I your God do understand,
the fragile frame of man.
As I depended upon my father for
all things I would have you to depend.

PETER

I did not want to get hurt, so I hid.
I put things off, so that I did not have to face them.
I hid myself, as a lamp under the table;
my screen was false humility and lies.

The light found me ashamed.
I had to surface under His relentless gaze.
As a potter he broke the resisting clay,
fashioning a new pot from the same.

I was a reed, bending under life's hurt and pain.
Now, in Gods truth, a Rock,

unbending and unashamed.

"And I tell you, you are Peter, and on this rock
I will build my church, and the gates of hell
shall not prevail against it." Matthew 16v18

EXPECTATIONS

The flower bowed, head dropped in shame,
 suffering a weathered look after a long hard
drought-
 It needed rain.

"Rise up my flower and look at me", said the Sun,
 seeing a life in need.
 Promising to pour a blessing forth;
 asking only it believes.

"Open your petals hide not your life within.

 Look into the face of love and I will pour my
blessing in".
 Rain came the very moment the petals opened.

"I will not disappoint your expectations", said the
Sun
"I shine forth upon my anointed one;
 will feed you that know a need,
 quenching your thirst with myself".

 I opened my hands as petals unfurled.
 I expect you to meet me, and I am never
disappointed.

A FRIEND

Lord, help me to be a friend:
A friend to those in need;
a friend to those who others despise,
unloved they mourn their past
and see no end.
Lord, they need a friend;
a friend who bears their burdens.
Who listens, but is not too quick to answer them.
Someone, instead of answers gives himself,
not fearing to speak the truth or
through fear of rejection, pretend.

As, you are my friend, my Lord,
unafraid of disclosure yet certain
of your Fathers love, so I desire your friendship,
Lord,
that I might be a friend to those who needs
someone
who loves them for themselves.

"A friend loves at all times." Proverbs 17v17

ANGEL BY A STREAM

I met an Angel by a stream;
like within a dream.
He held my hand
and walked with me
across the rising flood
of all my sin,
and for a time
I seemed weightless
as though no blood ran
within my veins.
Like an Angel
I had become.
He and I were one
for so short a time
as we crossed the spiritual line
between life and death.
Across life's barrier
and heaven above,
over turbulent water
and life's cold flood,
onto farther bank
where willows grow
And I shall know
a greater peace within
because my guardian Angel
guided me across
the flood of all my sin.

Now I'm free at last
to live my life again
without the burden
of my shame,
yet with an Angel's name,
and I shall know
a greater peace within
because my Angel
guided me across
the flood of all my sin.

TRUST

So simple is my daughter's trust,
so faithful is her pose,
straddling a climbing frame,
preparing to jump into daddy's arms;
trusting him not to let her fall.
I always am there to catch her;
save her from all harm.

Is my trust that simple?
Have I the faith to jump,
expecting Father God
to catch me as I fall?
Sometimes I feel that I have
no faith at all and would
not hear Him if He were to call.

"On this climbing frame of life
would you do less for your child
than I would do for you?
Would you really think that I
would encourage you to jump
only to drop my arms, letting you fall.
If I did that I would not
be a Father at all"

WEAK THINGS

My confidence is as delicate as a flower,
easily bruised, nerves easily opened.
Please speak tenderly to me,
quietly, as true love is spoken.
I cannot take too much,
not at this moment anyway.
Maybe later, when I have rested some,
my leaves angled to the sun and if you
my fellow traveller will come and spend some
time with me.
That will be enough and before the day has gone
maybe we can speak some more;
your sensitivity refreshing me-
Weak things need caring for.

"When the righteous cry for help, the Lord hears
and delivers them out of all their troubles. The
Lord is near to the broken hearted and saves the
crushed in Spirit. Many are the afflictions of the
righteous, but the Lord delivers him out of all of
them" Psalm 34v17-19

WHEN NIGHT TIME IS ENDED

I hear laughter like running water
streaming down a mountain face.
When will it end, when will it falter?
When time is folded up and we've run the race.

When starlight blinks out;
when night is no more
we will see more in that moment
than ever before.

When night time is ended;
when mornings begun
we'll sing a new song;
then we will be one.

HIGHEST CALLING

Yesterday was all too different from today.
Yesterday the storm clouds threatened.
Today, the sun with its many tendrils
search out the coldness of my heart,
sending its rays of heat deep down
into the darkness to light up the unreachable
places.
What trial is this; first the cold darkness,
the bitter conflict with this fallen nature,
the cold hostility for worldly power.
The tormenting aggression of invading troops
trying to make a bridgehead in my meagre
defences,
The unbounded light, the heart from which there
is no escape? The burning light of conviction that
immobilizes
my defensive screen.
The light shines in the darkness
and the darkness has not overcome it.
There is no change in my position,
for the Lord never changes.
There is only the question of allegiance
to the king; that is not in question.
So, I need to hold the higher ground,
the highest calling that He affords,
entrench myself within His love
and let His pleasure be my reward.

OVERCOMING

They shade my world,
these overhangs of unproductive gloom.
The sun through chinks of light
Attempts to reveal my room,

The room where I always come
when trouble shows its ugly head.
At times like this I sulk and brood
and wish that I were dead.

Even shadows cast their own shadows,
and beneath this canopy, so mean,
I sweat out all remorse and fears
for what might have been.

Yet through the gloom my spirit looms
as a knight with sword in hand,
wrestles to combat the gloom
and with his help to stand.

Chinks of light fall over me,
they cast out all my fears.
My knight has overcome the foe
and in my heart new hope appears.

MY ROCK, MY FORTRESS

I bend and bower with the wind, but do not break.

Trials of life seeks to throw me down.
I roll with the blow as a wrestler can
and lift my body to stall a winning move.
Turn my opponent in a reverse arm hold,
push to the canvas and force him down.

I may have been bowed but use that knowledge to
overcome.
To relinquish all thoughts of giving in
to pressures that will tie me down.

How I react to my circumstances make this man.
Should I yield when obstacles get in my way?
Or use them to find a better way?

I shall not break for God is by my side.
He is my strength when storms of life blow hard
and gives me hope when doldrums come by--

A Rock to lean upon where my soul abides.

FADING

Transparent has my life become-
Through me you can see the sun
Shining through the window pane
into my living room of pain!

Material things I'd cast aside
to know sweet peace inside!
All that I cared about has gone
like raindrops on a window
after the sun has come!

Maybe what I cared about was wrong
like a dark cloud crossing the sun,
blotting out for a time my life of care;
the sun has returned and no one's there.

No one there to answer when I call-
I feel so insignificant and small.
Today the sun shone through your eyes
and I was stripped of my disguise.

The mask I always held before my face
no longer there, it's in disgrace.
The sun shining through your kind eyes
has killed off pretence and lies.

Now I'm humbled by your grace
have found the will to seek your face
to open wide this heart of mine-

Filling it with glorious sunshine!

"Three times I pleaded with the Lord to take away from me. But he said to me, "My grace is sufficient for you, for my power is made perfect in weakness."

Therefore, I will boast all the more gladly about my weaknesses, so that Christ's power may rest on me"

2 Corinthians 12v8,9

LOVE YOURSELF

A storm arose within my heart.
I simply wanted to impart
a healing balm to my fellow man
held captive in this life's span.
The essence of what I held in my hand
was the power to understand.
Bad memories without wisdom's rein
can cause a lot of grief and pain.

    What started as a noble hope
    caused my mind not to cope.
    Quickly I lost my sense of worth;
    and capitulated to the earth.

Became a captive of the dark,
let visions and enchantment rule my heart.
So, I wallowed in my distress.
Badly needing renewed conquest.

    He came, a soldier from the war
    and taught me what I should be living for.
    United we now face the foe;
    inspired by love that only comrades know.

For alone I'd tried to gain the higher ground;
only sand is what I found.
For when your heart begins to fall
make sure there is someone to call.

    I tried my best to weather out the storm;
    only to end up beneath the foam.
    Loneliness seemed without end,

now at last I have a friend
who cares enough to risk drowning too.
That friend looking back at me is you.
The same old face, yet in the eyes
a look of triumph you can't disguise.
For, in the mirror, I see my face
and I no longer feel disgrace.
Simple pleasures are the best and at last,
I find my rest.
I'm glad I had this chat with you.
I pushed you aside for a while, was not true.
Yet you bided your time and gave me hope,
enough to make a little rope
to pull me from my lack of worth - I'm glad I learnt
to love myself.

SPARK

No mortal un-led can see the blessed spark
that rises, burning in the human heart
or know the peace that is sealed by fervent prayer.

Perplexed, I wonder how much I really care.
At times I think too much on our human state.
Is there more to sentient life than fate?
A quandary bears down fast upon me
like an avalanche of dire infamy.
Tis a dilemma rich for morbid thought;
could easily in a spider's web get caught

Must reflect some more on all things right
else lose direction in the dark of night.
Soul ignites through flint of hope,
helping me in this life to live and cope
with thoughts that too long dwell
    on the perplexities of heaven and hell.

NO PRETENCE

I found a friend-
A friend who lightens
my darkest moments.

Alone, I sit
and am less afraid now
than when no one was around
to dry my tears;
no one to share
my most thrilling moments;
deepest thoughts.

Everyone needs a friend,
otherwise, we would need
to pretend, invent a friend.
For that is what young children do.
My friend, I do not need
to pretend to you.

SMILE

Raise a smile,
how simple that would seem.
Only a smile,
two lips, a motion of the face,
so easy, requiring a happy heart;
that is where to start.

But when the heart is sad,
the future dim, we must meet life with a smile
and let the sunshine in.

'A happy heart makes the face cheerful,
  but heartache crushes the spirit.' Proverbs 15v13

SMALL FIRES

I hope I am fruitful,
do not just exist
in existence.

I am satisfied
as long as I am
producing.

It does not have
to be much to
be an inspiration.

We need small fires
lit by others
to encourage us
to light fires
of our own.

A ROSE BY MY BED

All seems so unreal.
Shattered and shaken my dreams
lying dead and still.

Was I mistaken to have put my trust
in someone I could not, see?
To put my faith in another,
supposedly higher than me?
Will I awake too soon to find
this was just a dream of mine?
Is what I am experiencing
only part of a dream, with little
sense or sign of reason?
Wake up, will you!
There is a rose by my bed.
It has a pink face.
It is such a little thing yet
such a gift as this means more to me
than all the promises left unfulfilled.
Lord, just a flower but in this tender thought
I am filled with renewed hope.
My faith in humanity watered
and given fresh energy to grow.

WINDFALL

The wind blows
and the great oak that has
stood these many ages at last falls.
The rot has set in.
Roots that had held its master
proudly aloft has given way;
and though it has lived a great age,
having seen many changes,
one more gust of wind was
more than enough, and it fell.

So ends a life,
having seen in life's book many pages;
now fallen to the earth that bore
him these many ages.

So, I have seen the sun rise and fall.
Having lived an eventful life
and given thanks and prayer.
The seed was planted and has grown
these many ages and when
my time has come to fall
let me have lived the life my
Master desires me to,
and fill his book of life
with many pages.

"I planted the seed, Apollos watered it, but God

has been making it grow. So, neither the one who plants not the one who waters is anything but only God, who makes things grow. The one who plants and the one who waters have one purpose, and they will each be rewarded according to their labour." 1 Corinthians 3v6

LOVE CONQUERS ALL

No shadows linger in my mind.
The sunlight today has been so kind.
For a time, storm clouds held the sun at bay
now your love has wiped my tears and fears away.

My heart no longer burdened by remorse
your love will guide me in life's course.
Rays of sunlight disperse all my mortal fear.
I know only love when you are near.

THE STAR OF BETHLEHEM

I saw a star shining brightly from afar-
The star of Bethlehem.
The light of divine peace giving my soul release-
The star of Bethlehem.

The creator of the sky, the earth, the sea
Came down to live His life in me-
The star of Bethlehem.

Love will never lose its glow,
If only shared will grow.
Brighter than the brightest star
That shone down on a manger from afar-

The star of Bethlehem.

UPON THEIR HEARTS

That my words were heart shaped.
Love un-transmitted lies dormant.
Love not given form in word or deed
lies drained and sad.

But love that's given leash.
That wells up from a heart of care
flows like a stream of healing
and comes forth as a prayer.

'I will put my law within them, and I
will write it upon their hearts' Jeremiah
31v33

UNDERSTANDING

I sit alone, thinking
in a hollow of land
between two hills-
they call it a valley-
but they don't understand.

They look and see
only problems and difficulties;
weeds and sand.
'A waste of time' they say.
'We are alright; let them find
 their own way!'

I look and see
flowers growing there;
encouraged by love
and tender care.
Nourished by relentless prayer.

Understanding grows best
in difficulty and darkness;
as roots out of a dry ground.

RESURRECTION

There seems no shadow anymore,
they have dispersed
like so many times before
when the sun has risen
and challenged their domain;
no longer will they come again.

Only if allowed to come,
out of weakness yet undefined,
encroaching on my life like a noise,
dissipating harmony,
creating discord, not a song.

Yet the sun has come
and with its life and heat
harmony is restored-

There is left only a sense of peace.

LET NOT YOUR HEART GROW WEARY

Let not your heart grow weary,
let not your love grow cold,
for it is I, your Lord, who love you and leads you.
Let not your love grow cold.

For I, your Lord, who is the strength of your life.
Let not your love grow cold.
For in Me you have life abundantly;
to me you are more precious than gold.

Cast off your fears for the future,
your cares for the days of your life.
Take up my cross, follow me each day;
therein is death to all strife.

Put on my garment of mercy,
my garments of praise and of love.
Then you will neither be cold or weary;
your heart will be full of my love.

'Put on then, as Gods chosen ones, holy and
beloved,
compassion, kindness, lowliness, meekness and
patience. And above all these things put on love.'

Colossians 3v12

INTO THE LAND

Reach out to me and hold my hand
and we will walk into the Land,
where the air is clean, my Son has been;
only come with open hands.

There is abundance there.
Enough for all, and then to spare.
All that's good, all that's right,
only, be prepared to fight.

Many Giants there are, all defeated by the Son,
rely as they do on deceit and fear:
Stand firm in Jesus, watch them run.

I reach out to you and hold your hand.
The ground I stand upon no longer sand
but rock, firm and stable.
All things in you I do, am able.

'If you falter in times of trouble,
 how small is your strength.' Proverbs 24v10 NIV

THE ARMS OF THE LORD

Love takes the initiative.
It is not slow to do good.
Before it is asked it acts.
Its response is always pleasing.

It does not look for personal gain
but sacrifices itself for the sake of others.
God is love, we are the arms of the Lord
which His love moves unconditionally through.

UNTO US A CHILD IS BORN
To Katherine Anne our daughter born 7/1/84

I am glad I awoke to find the difference.
The difference in the smell of air.
The difference in a humble prayer.
A difference that a smile can bring.
The difference when Spring begins.
When new life begins as crocuses
through the melting snow.
So dies my winter fears, so lives today
A promised child, so dear.
For unto us a child is born.

'Rain, in abundance, O God, thou didst shed
abroad; thou didst restore their heritage as it
languished; thy flock
 found a dwelling in it; in there, O God, thou didst
provide for the needy' Psalm 68v9,10

GOD IS SO BIG

I feel so small compared to You,
so large when compared to me,
so inadequate when compared
to all my problems.
Yet if I saw them as You see them
Then how small they would be.
How silly I am when I am in Your hands
to worry about the things that worry me.

'My sheep hear My voice, and I know them,
And they follow Me,' and I give them eternal life;
and they shall never perish, and no-one shall
snatch them out of my hand.' John 10v27, 28

THERE ARE ALWAYS GIANTS

'The land is over there: Can you see it?'
Hills rising up into the sky, great fortress cities
and vineyards.
A land rich and overflowing with promise:
'Yet look, there are Giants!'
Giants guarding the outskirts of this abode.
Amorites and Nephilim-sin and fear combine
to destroy the word of faith that God has spoken.

'See, the Lord your God has given you the land.
You must go in and take possession of it as the
Lord,
the God of your fathers told you.'

'Do not be discouraged or afraid, for the Lord, your
God is with you.'
Yet thcy were afraid, and they were discouraged.
They threw the blame on their leaders and the
Lord.
The land was theirs for the taking yet they ended
up walking in the wilderness for forty more years.
They believed not Gods word.
That generation never came into the land.
We need to walk in and take it – but there are
Giants. There will always be Giants that bar our
way into Gods Holy presence.
Goliath was the difference between victory and
defeat to the Israelites yet he was bowled over by a

PHILIP CARMEN

small round stone from a slingshot aimed by only a boy who had some fear of him- Yet David feared God more.

ALWAYS WITH YOU

Daddy, please leave the door open,
for I'm so afraid of the dark.
When you go to bed you will come to see me?
You will tuck me in?
And please leave the door open to let the light in.

Father, please let your light in!
Please keep the door open
for I am afraid of the dark.
I need to know you are near me,
to love and to cheer me, to hear caring
words softly spoken.

Son, the door to your heart you need to keep open.
My light will always shine and cast out all sin and
fear.
You need to trust me for I am always near
and before a word is spoken, I will answer your
prayers.
You always will be my beloved:

I, your Father, will always care.

'And surely, I am with you always,
 to the very end of the age' Matthew 28v20

SPEAK TO YOURSELF

Rise up my soul, how low you have fallen.
Your opinion of yourself dropped to zero.
You have nothing left to be satisfied with.
You have failed this time, like the other times
yet each time you sink further into
disillusionment.
What will become of you?

You will arise and put His Holy garment on.
His praise to wear as a mantle;
to lift the burden of sadness from off your
shoulders.
For His Grace is sufficient for you;

as long as you relinquish your life for His.

LIVING SEED

"Why does the sun shine in the forest glade no
more?"
"Is it because we have let the small saplings grow,
the bindweed, bramble and the seeds they sow
along
 the pathway and beneath the trees?"

"Which is the way to go, Lord, tell me please?"
"The way has become so dark, my progress so
slow,
   can I possibly go on when I am hindered so?"
"Lord, tell me please, for the day is nigh gone,
   and the forest is darker, I need you more
   than ever to depend upon."

 In that very moment a ray of insight glinted
 through the shadows and myriad of leaves.
 The Lord spoke into my innermost being.
"Cut a way through the forest, there are paths
through the trees,
   prepare the ground around you and plant living
seed"

I HAVE A FRIEND

I have a friend whose name is God.
His love will never end, He is my friend.

The future holds no fear to me for Jesus
holds me in His hands and in His hands is victory.
His perfect love casts out all fear and He is near
me.
I have a friend who is faithful, true and kind.
He teaches me to seek and find.
He is a friend in whom I can depend.
I can be myself and not pretend.

I have a friend whose name is God.
His love will never end, He is my friend.

'So, lying thus, close to the breast of Jesus' John
13v25

WHEN NIGHT TIME IS ENDED

I hear laughter like running water
streaming down a mountain face.
When will it end, when will it falter?
When time is folded up and we've run the race.

When starlight blinks out.
When night is no more
we will see more in that moment
than ever before.

When night time is ended.
When mornings begun
we'll sing a new song then
and we will be one.

'Lo! I tell you a mystery. We shall not all sleep,
but we shall all be changed, in a moment, in the
twinkling of an eye, at the last trumpet. For the
trumpet will sound, and the dead will be raised
imperishable, and we shall be changed. For the
perishable nature must put on the imperishable,
and this, mortal nature must put on immortality.'
1 Corinthians 15v51-54

SPEAK TO YOURSELF

Rise up my soul, how low you have fallen.
Your opinion of yourself dropped to zero.
You have nothing left to be satisfied with.
You have failed this time like all the others
yet each time you sink further into
disillusionment.
"What will become of you?"

You will arise and put His holy garments on.
Praise to wear as a mantle to lift the burden
of sadness from off your shoulders
for His grace is sufficient for you --

As long as you relinquish your life for His.

"Once God has spoken; twice have I heard this:
that power belongs to God; and that to thee, O Lord
belongs steadfast love; for thou dost requite a man
according to his work." Psalm 61v11, 12

LIFE HAS A WAY OF GOING ON

Life has to go on
like a 'well remembered' song
Never quite forgotten
but so seldom sung.

When disappointment threatens
and doubts through crannies
and cracks creep in
we need to remember
the good things God has done.
To see through craggy clouds,
the sun.

Though grief for a moment
may hide our Lords face
His love is constant,
he is never dismayed.

Loss by death threatens to strip
life's fabric away
yet still God goes on loving,

His goodness unchanging,

though our hearts might stray.

THE OLD DARK CHURCH

The old dark church stands on its own
on a bare portion of hillside, atop a ridge of trees.
Around it an ancient graveyard,
older than the church itself,
on the cold hilltop with a view
of fresh ploughed fields.

None can remember the age of the low flint wall
or the yews growing either side of the rustic gate.

'Yews hold demon forces at bay' so the parish
legends say.
Those who think they are wiser intrude at their
peril
on death's deep longing for privacy

.

THE JUGGLER

The juggler keeps coloured balls in the air.
They must not be seen to fall,
he keeps them there.
His secret is to find a rhythm,
then with careful balance
and practiced skill he keeps them there-
Passing them from hand to hand,
through the air
The juggler is a lot like you and me.
We both have too many things
going on at one time
yet we accomplish very little one can see.
As long as we are causing the impression
that everything is fine we are accomplishing
all we can in kind.

So easy is it for us to acquire a skill,
so, proving we are in control.
But Jesus says that there is a better way,
if only we could give the control of our lives away.
Not trying to hold an audience
with our own special skill
but trusting in Jesus our lives to fulfil.
So, I reach out to Him with open hands,
neither clinging onto one vestige of self-interest
nor manipulating others as we so easily can;
only coming to Jesus and letting

the balls roll out of my hands.

CHRIST THE ROCK

Christ is the rock, on which I stand,
all other ground is sinking sand.
The rock on which my hope is hung
is shelter from the growing storm?

The rest I sought is hidden deep
in the caring heart that will never sleep.
Myself may fade but through His death
a rose there grows, eternal life.

Hardness of heart gives way to His true love;
all fear and strife now cease to live.
For I believe that He now lives
to free us from our selfish pride
and share the love that He doth give.

"Simon, son of John, do you love me? John 21v6

THE SHEPHERD

His saving grace is there to keep
a watch over His grazing sheep
and when in trouble or in pain
he soothes them with His Holy name.
just like a shepherd with His crook;
guiding those who at Him look.

"The Lord is my shepherd; I shall not want" Psalm
23v1

SOMEONE MUST HAVE PRAYED

Someone has placed their hand in mine;
sensing that the best is yet to come,
that the valley shadows lingering still
only enhance the morning as it comes
rushing from behind the hill: the sun.
And all that seemed so frightening
the night before, clinging like cobwebs,
strands of deception were unveiled,
revealing nothing but my fears
lying harmless now that God
with his sword of truth has cut,
dealt with so decisively.

Someone who loves me must have prayed.
Someone who loves me is praying still.

"The Lord is far from the wicked but he hears the
prayer of the righteous" Proverbs 15v29
"In the same way, the Spirit helps us in our
weakness." Romans 8v26

RESOLVE

They rush at me

with banshee, screaming voices.
Rush relentlessly as the tide,
scorning mouths open wide;
filling with every step the
broad expanse of nothingness.

I await my fortuitous fate.
Limbs manacles to the ground with fear;
heart pounding out of control
like a tortured deer.

One who comes before the rest,
harbouring hate within his stare
stops fast when faced by my resolve;
evaporates into air.

Silent terrors of the night,
lonely torments of the day
evaporate like the morning mist
the instant that I pray.

NO CONDEMNATION

When I have seen thee
heavy tread
the path
that sought
to condemn
a man
for being wrong,
so, lose a friend.

I would rather
take upon me
all his blame
and meekly tread
the path he trod
for even so
it led to God
and left its
scars and pain
on Calvary.

"The Lamb who is at the heart of the throne will be
their shepherd and will guide them to the spring
of the water of life." Revelations 7v17

ISAIAC (YIELDING)

This child, he's mine by right.
You gave him to me so why, I ask
when the time is so near, must he die?

If you will not yield his life to me:
His life is mine by right:
Can I not do with him what I need to do?
Do you not trust me to fulfil that which
I have said will come to pass and even now
withhold what is good that the better may be?

I yield my ways that yours may flourish and bear
fruit,
yielding up the one precious thing I have that I
might gain
more of you and in so doing gain all besides-

My Isaiac on Mount Moriah

'Verily, verily, I say unto you, except a corn of
wheat fall into the ground and die, it abides alone;
but if it die, it brings forth much fruit' John 12v24
'He, who did not spare his own son, but gave him
up for us. Now will he not also along with him,
graciously give us all things' Romans 8v32

A SERVICEMAN

He sits upon a rock,
a soldier looking out to sea,
his path is set, mind renewed,
all power is his, the plan is sure;
calm the tide of future ills.

No longer does he guard his fate.
Another's he is by right.
A civilian no more but a serviceman,
enlisted he is to fight the fight.

I am that serviceman,
afraid but trusting all the same.
My feet are set firm upon a rock,
I bear my Saviour's name.

This evil tide must break its back
before its final throes,
For I, safe upon this rock
know what it does not.

No wave can shake me loose,
for my Master controls the sea.
So, I can rest myself in Him
and He can live His life through me.

YOUR WAY, LORD

Lord, I am still chasing after who I am.
The race I'm running is away from confrontation.
Where do I fit into life, into the scheme of things?
Only as I face up to life will I find my place in life;
the place God has for me.
The purpose He wants to fulfil through me.
Lord, you said,' Perfect love casts out fear.'
And 'I am the strength of your life.'

'You are my rock and my salvation; who shall I fear?'
'You are the strength of my life, of who shall I be afraid?'

Your ways are different from my ways.
Your pathway to maturity is not the pathway I would choose.
Bend my pathway Lord to converge with Yours.
Bend my will to submit to Your will.
For only in doing Your will is there security.
Only in obedience to Your Word, given in love, will I not be afraid.

'As many as received him; to them gave he the power to become the Sons of God' John 1v12

THE SONG OF CHRIST

Lord, save me from singing a song
I should not sing.
The bird in the treetop sings
a song made for it to sing.

It is beauty as the song
It sings is beautiful.
I will eventually become
the image of my song;

Eventually become as meaningful
as the song I sing and as the bird
will await the dawning of a new day
with a joy that amounts to splendour
upon the tree of my surrender.

I await the morning,
when the morning comes
and will share with human kind
the song upon my tongue.

'Christ wants to live His life in us
and fulfil His will through us' Galatians 2v20

DOUBT

Today I was cast adrift
into the proximity of a whirlpool of doubts.
Doubts that picked holes in a
patchwork quilt of experience;
that undid stitches that I thought
would never wear out.

Stitches of divine healing literally laid bare.
All that I had relied upon;
all that I had read about,
depended on, successfully
stitched into other people's fabrics.
Fool-proof or so I thought.

Now I must think again on
the material that I had bought,
for that which I had relied upon,
now laid bare to the barest seams.
I must pick away until
I've picked self-glory out.
Until all that's left is Christ
and Christ is all to me.

My work of art is pulled to shreds,
What is left is only regal thread,
and God must sow His love therein
and I must die to sin.

"And Jesus answered them, Truly, I say to you,

if you have faith and do not doubt,
you will not only do what has been done to the fig
tree,
but even if you say to the mountain, be taken up
and thrown into the sea, it will happen," Matthew
21v21

SERVANT KING

Their Saviour hangs limp upon a cross,
vital signs so quickly falling.
Chill wind of rejection blows,
Mary, his mother is crying.

Disciples stand dejected beneath the cross.
Instinctively feel his dire agony and pain;
Immobilised with the sadness of his loss,
Know humiliation and deepest shame.

Only the previous week they sat around a table.
Saw him break bread, share it around.
He washed their feet, dried it with his hair,
Called them to be servants; no king was crowned.

This passion should have been a celebration.
Now one felt like some simple fool.
All that they had believed now torn apart-
What King rules from a servant's stool?

The sky grew angry, dark upon the hillside,
thunder roared and lightning struck a tree,
Their Master lifted His head and cried,
'Father, why have you forsaken me?'

'But not my will but thine be done!'
Then their Saviour died on Calvary.

His followers cried out in grief and fear.
Peter comforted a grieving Mary.

Miracles were seen that night
from Jerusalem to Jericho.
People blind from birth could now see.
Iscariot's shame hung from a Judas tree.

Death was dark, no subtle shade of grey.
What mystery there lay was hidden deep within
Joseph of Arimathea's tomb.
A large boulder rolled across so not to let intruders
in.

Yet, this place called Gethsemane
was not to be His last resting place.
Pure rivers of life run from his wounds still
and everlasting life is given by Grace.

"The greatest among you will be your servant."
Matthew 23v11

GIVING OURSELVES

I grow it in a garden though I did not see it grow,
before I knew you my world was full of weeds,
there was no room for your fruit of love to grow.
But you took me by the hand and planted me in
your garden.

There are still weeds but by your love they will not
thrive
and fill again the ground that you have hoed.
You trust me Lord to keep your garden free from
weeds that flower and sow.

So, in your garden I grow free to bear the fruit you
require of me; and as you send down showers of
blessings my love for you will never lessen but
increase and grow.
As joy brings strength to weary limbs and love
being
the fruit of suffering through weather perverse
and stormy yet will I not hold my fruit to me but
share your fruit of love abundantly.

Sharing with others who need to know the grace
of God to help them grow, and need someone who
cares enough to show that love to them by giving
themselves as an offering!

REDEMPTION

"Call me a fool if you like!"
I could see the future in the stars
telling me which fool to strike.
"Do you not feel remorse?"
My heart is still pounding in my chest.
I need to refrain from this evil course
before it becomes manifest.

Someone cradles me in His hands,
telling me, in His promises, I must stand.
For I was locked in bitterness
yet now hold the key, forgiveness.
Some discordant voice has said,
"You were given false promises,
   and was much too easily led"

Yet, I know that as a lie,
filtered into the farthest
reaches of my head
and I would simply rather die
than believe the lie that Evil said.
I must stay close to you, Lord of Light
for you have made sure that I'm alright
and are readying me for the fight
that is sure to come.

Through the misty night
when shades come forth on black horses,

eyes shining demonic bright;
must cut them down with Truths sword of light.

After the final trumpet sound
when at last this War is won
and I am with the Holy One,
my sins forgiven by the son,
giver of peace and light.
knowing that God's Word is always right.

COMING BACK

Coming back to one who clings,
I am being drawn by loves unfailing strings.
The One who draws has immortal power,
cannot fail to draw me in.
I have a choice, to submit or cower;
to resist and sin or lose my heart to Him!

For I am coming home as the prodigal,
back to His Fathers care.
I have failed but now take steps
to pave my way to Him in prayer!

I have tasted the loneliness of living for myself.
Now I seek Gods holiness, for with Christ alone
there's wealth.
And I crave no longer indulging in myself.

The Father runs to meet His son; embarrassed in
His arms.
He holds my heart from harm and I in Him am
one.
Ready am I to settle down, settling for no other
call
than that which I now own- no sedimentary port
of call,
but his immortal throne.

"But it was appropriate to celebrate and be glad,
for this, your brother, was dead, and is alive again.

He was lost, and is found." The Prodigal Son Luke
15v32

NOT ONLY NOW

I don't thank you only
for your goodness now
but in the midst of pain,
thank you for your enduring power,
that tender heart that
held this feeble hand whose
squeeze I feel even now
as I sit where others have set before,
enveloped in that smile of yours
and wonder how you love me so,
how,

      how
         and how?

SHADOWS IN THE NIGHT

Etched upon my consciousness
a simple trick of mind's duress.
In the darkness of the night
spirits moved into my sight.
Visions of sinister harm,
striking with unerring charm,
unearthing fears I could not face,
moved my madness more apace.
A hole opened like a creature's jaw
and I was sucked into its gaping maw.
Projected as from a loaded gun,
I fell into a place that good men shun.
Falling, falling with little sense of time,
a prison sentence for my crime.
All fibre of my being held me enthral,
condemned me forever to fall.

Then a glorious light filled my gloom,
I awoke in my own room.
Now conscious of my mortal plight,
I shunned the torments of night,
laid hold of my immortal soul,
prised myself from that damned hole.
Since sunlight did awaken me,
I see the route of simplicity;
the taunts of a troubled mind
can harbour demons of a kind.

Rest assured I will not sleep;

I have an appointment to keep.
The sun has filled my tortured mind
now all fear has lifted and I find
that shadows cast upon a painted wall
can in the night make you fall.
Reflections in the corner of your eye
can burn away the heart of all desire.

It would please the Devil to intrude,
fit me for his evil brood,
but light obliterates fancies of the night
making my heart and mind alright.

ST JOHNS CROSS, WINCHESTER

Suffused with an incense of divine peace;
set within ancient flint and brick walls
time seems to stand still.

Clothed in holy raiment
timelessness is instilled
through ambience of a holy place;
soaked in healing balm.
Protected from the world
by an alliance with the Maker
of heaven and earth.

In the garden a carp pond
with lily pads and flowing fountains
and an ancient oak with dovecot
impress itself upon a modern brain
that here is a sanctuary of peace,
indeed tranquillity, even in this world of change.
Nothing changes here.
Alms houses built for the poor
almost a millennium ago.
The gate keeper still gives out the
travellers dole of ale and bread
that they have given since the Middle Ages.

Once John Keats walked around these
antiquated halls and sensed a peace
within the genius of his soul.

Here he wrote his famous 'autumn' poem
sitting within the sanctity of St. John Cross.
Divine inspiration, some might say, burnt within
him.

Shirley and I sit holding hands,
sharing an experience of garden bliss,
enveloped in natures maternal arms,
resting in Gods Holy tryst;

safe for a time from harm.

GOD IS SO BIG!

I feel so small compared to You Lord-
So large when compared to me,
so inadequate when compared
to all my problems
yet if I saw them as you see them
then how small they would be.

How silly I am when I am in your loving hands
to worry about everything that worries me?

LIFE ETERNAL

The Sun doth rise
It heals me now,
my wounds are sealed
with heat of prayer.

But when Sun sets,
"What healing then?"
Life eternal for all men!

NATIVITY

Another year over, another year;
a new year to come-
What of the old?
What treasure have I opened now that Christmas
is here?

Let me see --- The manger lies alone
and uninviting to a natural eye;
yet a supernatural one beckons – "Come in."

The new has come. A place to be born,
a place to stretch and know his parents' love.
I know that love; a love that does not crush
but encourages me to grow.

A father's love – strict but tirelessly devoted,
A mother's love – tender and sacrificial,
moulded upon the wheel of inhospitable times,
yet pure as gold, fashioned for a king.

What has the year brought forth?
What will the New Year bring?

New fruit- One hopes so.
Virtue disclosed, humility born out of suffering,
obedience out of belonging.

To know Jesus as my Lord and king,
as His servant follow Him.
To simply let go of all besides
that hinders my knowing Him.

A dying to ambition, letting go of self-esteem;
relinquishing of an earthly throne.

A simple manger,
a simple birth,
a simple choice
to make in the years ahead.

To die that man might be forgiven.
To live that man may no more die.

"Today in the town of David a Saviour has been
born to you; he is the Messiah, the Lord. This will
be a sign to you: You will find a baby wrapped in
swaddling clothes and lying in a manger" Luke 2 v
10, 11

A GARDEN PARADISE

In our garden paradise I see
life is good for you and me.
It is years since we laid our garden down
from scrawl upon well- worn parchment, brown.

Each bed was shaped to meet the sun,
rising in the morn, when days begun.
Between the beds, a rye grass lawn
laid out in love, as fresh hopes are born.

To hear a child at play upon the grass
is sweeter than nectar from a glass.
From babe in arms to child at play
affected us so profoundly in a life changing way.

A bubbling fountain blesses the ear
like nothing else that we can hear.
A pond with goldfish swimming round
creates pure harmony so profound.

In our multi-coloured garden rockery
I remember troubles that once plagued me.
Yet without the trouble that shaped my soul
I would not in the end have been made whole.

A hydrangea bush in summer view
sets the scene for all we do.
We sit beneath our cherry tree
and marvel at nature's rich tapestry.

We placed a dove cot in our tree
to enhance our sense of tranquillity.
Last of all we set the sundial;
this gives our garden antique style.

Sitting, reflecting on our patio
life has been richer for the things we sow.
From blessed blooms to childish laughter
we have no fear of what comes after.

For after life I shall simply see
a paradise garden bloom for you and me.
In that eternal place of love
we can trust our father God above

to keep us from a troubled mind
that paves the path of all mankind.
Never alone while I sit in garden bliss
and know a tender lover's kiss.

My garden is a place of lasting hope
that helps me through my life to cope.

Now in the autumn days of care
I thank my God in heartfelt prayer
for allowing me life and harmony
among the flowers and creatures that I see.

Life is abundant for those who care
enough to give their heart to prayer
for others who need a place of peace
and find in a garden their soul's release.

THE TREE IS GREEN

'Why do I still cry?'
My roots go deep into Gods love
and I have reached the place that
I must make him my all.
For you see, growing means dependency;
and I see the fruit upon the tree,
yet the tree is green, the bark is tender still.

But as my branches grow,
stretching out for all to know;
they cannot choose whom to approach,
and who not to approach.
Love calls to give a hand to all that grow in Zions
land.

And though someone is different though
strong in their area of influence.
'Why do I flinch and fail to meet?'
He is as I, a son, dependant on the holy one.
My tree is green; the bark is tender still.

But see, he holds out his hand to me.
To meet his touch would only be
reaching across my inferiority and take his hand.
We have different roles to play but both
are written into Gods own perfect plan.

We need to work together.
He holds my key and I hold his.

We have not the right to withhold and not to give.
My tree has aged, is brown,
my branches wear a leafy crown,

and I have no need to pretend to you, my friend-
Love always gives, it never lends.

'At least there is hope for a tree. If it is cut down, it
will sprout again, and the new shoots will not fail.'
Job 14v7

WORTH

There is a semblance of reality
that time and again one must face down.
A facile interpretation of mediocracy
as an elusive ephemeral spirit
disappears down unmarked streets
one has never seen or been before.
So crestfallen has my mundane life become-
This sedimentary life that I wished I'd lived.

Maybe, after all, this is some deep longing
of a man longing to recapture his youth!

At this moment in time there is no secret panacea
that can possibly help me escape from this
moment in time,
only to escape down a dark languid tunnel of
obscure absurdity!

Are these stark and folded memories that haunt
me
only just some patchwork quilt stitched together
out of vacant dreams?
Why am I feeling so ambivalent to my own scarred
sense of worth?
A sad old life wasted by incessant thought purging
all
that could have been so very good.

I must accept all that I am; all that I am deemed to

be;
a worthy soul battered but not broken by
the tempestuous tides of his own history.

SOMETHING STIRS BENEATH THE SEA

Somewhere, something stirs beneath the sea.
Perhaps it is the shipwreck of who I used to be.
A faded relic of a shambolic past that
through Gods pity was allowed to last.

To last through the tangled seaweed in my mind,
eking out any existence it could find
within hidden crevices one can try to hide,
trying to escape the seas ruthless tide
that brings destruction in its wake
as well as lost desire and heartache.

Somewhere, something stirs down deep within
that harboured once my mortal sin.
Something I no longer wish to hide,
this mortal fear and horrid pride.

I so need, Lord, your peace to dwell inside;
your perfect peace, love and rest
so that I can really know that I am blessed.

The sea within is calm today.
Your love has driven worry far away.
You walk upon the water still;
calming my soul and all that was ill.

Purpose has come, making its presence known.
Out of tragedy my once ill-fated life has grown.

Now I must somehow impart
these lessons learnt through dark of night;
bring blessing to another person's heart.

Together we can overcome and do what's right.

'And they have overcome him by reason of the
blood of the Lamb, and by reason of the word of
their testimony; and they loved not their lives
unto the death.' Revelation 12 v11

SOUL TO SOUL

I belong to the land
and to the rolling sea,
whose gentle undulations
are part of me.

The hills that rise
like a woman's breast
from forces deep
within mother earth
that gave it birth.
Birds know the perfect time
to build their nest
and are duly blest.

The sea that
ebbs and flows-
Only the sun and moon know
life's tension between the spheres
that prolong our O so fragile lives
through the rolling expanse
of all our years.

I lift my head from my lover's bed
where burdens of today now are shed.
I feel as one with the land,
sea, moon and sun.
Our lives entwine like the vine,
bearing precious fruit in their time.

Two lovers,
body and soul entwine.
Knowing fulfilment from loves
sweet sacrificial wine.

We all belong to the land
and to the rolling sea.
Our lives linked intrinsically;
as it was always meant to be.
Soul to searching soul,
you are the reason I am whole.
We are part of the moon, sun, land and sea-

Only in you am I truly me.

THE SUN

The sea is lost in shadow,
the sky is not yet one
with the sea and land
for all await the sun.

It rises in the east
when morning shadows wane
and sky, sea and land
give praise again.

LIFE ETERNAL

The Sun doth rise
It heals me now.
My wounds are sealed
with heat of prayer.

But when Sun sets,
'What healing then?'
Life eternal
for all men.

HELD CAPTIVE

They closed the door.
I was locked within
a room which kept
resentment in.

The door was locked.
I had the key.
Forgiveness dwelt
inside of me.

I open wide the door.
One word it takes.
Love opens any door-
I need not hate.

"For if you forgive people their trespasses Your
heavenly Father will also forgive you" Matthew
6v14 Mark 11v25

SENSE OF WORTH

Can this be life when all I do and all I say
is passed aside like new mown hay?
And can it be that I alone am skittered
across life's lake like a stone?
Of no value, and even less credit due?

Would someone say when I am gone?
"He was a credit to us, his always was a job well
done".
I wonder who, I wonder who?

Yet I cry out for something new.
Somehow there must be more than this.
Will at the end of the day find
that I have missed my way
and walked in only half the truth;
even worse find my sense of worth
Shattered like fallen crockery upon
the shelf of ignominy?

Answer: "Why are you feeling down?
There is so much to be thankful for.
There is so much water in the world
without your tears adding to it.
Laughter is what the world needs
and hears so little of.

Compassion for those worse off than yourself
is far more precious than the fading

flower of deep regret;
the dried-up water hole of self-pity;
belying a state of raw neglect.

Let the water be streams of love
flowing from an eternal source,
down into the hearts of all humanity;
reconciling these embittered fragments
whole to God.

FAITH

Look, there is land ahead:
Safe passage for my feet to tread.

This waters much too difficult to walk upon.
The sea alters with every wave formed.
Swell is contrary, I am not brave;
no stability, wave upon wave.
The sea is an adventure, land is a slave.
Faith is a song continuing on.
Doubt is unyielding, unfruitful and staid.

Land is for settling, settling down.
Water for moving onward, exploration-

Sanctified ground.

AN ANSWER

World sentient,
garden innocent;
God reliant,
man pliant.

Snake disarming,
holiness harming,
deceit effective,
humankind defective.

Woman ashamed,
man blamed;
temptation known,
evil sown.

Woman frigid,
man livid.
Heart falling,
God calling;
no one listening,

Sacrifice needed,
garden weeded.
Only son bled
in human-kinds stead.

Freedom of choice,
let's rejoice.

Never again presume
garden will bloom.

Compassion to be the soil,
never let fruit spoil.
Faith is the key,
only hope, humility
for you and me.

No one can separate,
man must God imitate:

Say no to hate.

MY HANDS

These hands of mine
they hold in them
the capacity to bring
healing to all men.

The power to withhold
and not to give
rests in my hands
that they might not live.

The power to hold
and bring some care
into the hearts of men
alive with fear.

These hands of mine
connected to a heart of care
desires to bring hope
to humanity everywhere.

ENCOURAGE ME

Please encourage me.
I need a helping hand.
Just a word will do.

Please try to understand,
just as a tender plant
needs the rain
I need refreshing too.

"encourage the faint hearted, help the weak,
 be patient with them all" 1 Thessalonian 5v14

LIVING SEED

"Why does the sun shine in the forest glade no
more?"
"Is it because we have let the small saplings grow,
  The bindweed, bramble and the seeds they sow
along
  the pathway and beneath the trees?"

"Which is the way to go, Lord, tell me please?"

"The way has become so dark, my progress so
slow,
  can I possibly go on when I am hindered so?"
"Lord, tell me please, for the day is nigh gone,
  and the forest is darker, I need you more
  than ever to depend upon."

  In that very moment a ray of insight glinted
  through the shadows and myriad of leaves.
  The Lord spoke into my innermost being.

"Cut a way through the forest, there are paths
through the trees, prepare the ground around you
and plant living seed."

"This is my Fathers glory, that you bear much
fruit,
  showing yourselves to be my disciples." John
15v8

POWER WHEN THE SPIRIT COMES

There is a sound, a sound of rushing waters
coming from the mountain, flowing to the valley
and filling all people with gladness.
The people are filled with awe at the waters
coming
like a mighty river rushing down the mountain,
Filling up the valley and bringing life to an arid
land.
Deserts become meadowland where our sheep and
cattle graze.
So, providing food for the people of the land which
our Lord God had promised--

Changing their hunger into feasting and their
mourning into dancing--

Pray to the Lord your God for the land to bring
increase.
Pray again for the turtle dove to sing in the land.

A land that God has promised to give His sons and
daughters as an inheritance--
Pray for peace to be in the land. The Lord will grant
you peace.
Pray for holiness to increase. The Lord requires a
holy people uncontaminated
by the wickedness of sin: a special and peculiar
people to Him.

Pray that His Spirit shall flow like a river.
Pouring forth within the hearts of men, bringing
life to a thirsty land-

Healing to all nations on this Earth.

'But you shall receive power when the Holy Spirit
has come upon you; and you shall be my witnesses
in Jerusalem and in all Judea and Samaria and to
the end of the earth.'

'There leaves will not wither nor their fruit fail,
but they will bear fresh fruit every month, because
the water for them flows from the sanctuary.
Their fruit will be for food, and their leaves for
healing.' Ezekiel 47v12

COMING BACK

Coming back to one who clings,
I am being drawn by loves unfailing strings.
The One who draws has immortal power,
cannot fail to draw me in;
I have a choice, to submit or cower;
to resist and sin or lose my heart to Him.

For I am coming home as the prodigal.
Back to His Fathers care.
I have failed but now take steps
to pave my way to Him in prayer.
I have tasted the loneliness of living for myself,
now I seek Gods holiness, for with Christ alone
there's wealth
and I crave no longer indulging in myself.

The Father runs to meet His son, I fall
embarrassed into His arms.
He holds my heart from harm and I in Him am
one.
Ready am I to settle down, settling for no other
call
than that which I now own- no sedimentary port
of call,
but His immortal throne.

"But it was appropriate to celebrate and be glad,
for this, your brother, was dead, and is   alive

again. He was lost, and is found." The Prodigal Son
Luke 15v32
"He heals the broken hearted and binds up their
wounds" Psalm 147v3

SPEAK TO YOURSELF

Rise up my soul, how low you have fallen.
Your opinion of yourself dropped to zero.
You have nothing left to be satisfied with.
You have failed this time, like the other times
yet each time you sink further into
disillusionment.
'What will become of you?'

You will arise and put His Holy garments on.
His praise to wear as a mantle,
to lift the burden of sadness
from off of your shoulders;
His Grace is sufficient for you,
as long as you relinquish your life for His.

'Once God has spoken; twice have I heard this: that
power belongs to God; and that to thee, O Lord,
belong steadfast love. For thou dost requite a man
according to his work.' Psalm 61v11, 12

THE SHEPHERD

His saving grace is there to keep
a watch over His grazing sheep
and when in trouble or in pain
He soothes them with His Holy name.
Just like a shepherd with His crook-

Guiding those who at Him look.

"The Lord is my Shepherd, I shall not want." Psalm
23v1

STARS

There is nothing that seems so right
than watching stars at night;
Nothing that moves my heart so much;
to me they are so much more than lights
against a screen of darkness!

I wonder at the breadth of vision
to create this vast panoramic motion picture
that moves on endlessly to infinity;
filling all, who take the time to look, with wonder!

How can people look, yet do not see that
the same God who created what I now see,
created you and me!

"He determines the number of the stars; he gives
to all of them their names." Psalm 147v4
"When I look at your heavens, the work of your
fingers, the moon and the stars, which you have
set in place, what is man that you are mindful of
him, and the son of man that you care for him?"
Psalm 8v3-4

INTO THE LAND

Reach out to me and hold my hand
and we will walk into the Land,
where the air is clean, my son has been;
only come with open hands.

There is abundance there,
enough for all, and then to spare.
All that's good, all that's right;
only, be prepared to fight.

Many Giants there are, all defeated
by the son, relying as they do on deceit and fear-
Stand firm in Jesus, watch them run.

I reach out to you and hold your hand.
The ground I stand upon no longer sand
but rock, firm and stable:
All things in you I do, am able.

"If you falter in times of trouble, how small is your
strength." Proverbs 24v10 NIV

REJOICE IN THEM ALL

Miles and miles of stony beaches,
walking thoughtfully along the seas edge;
throwing stones at the waves
as they lap inexorably shoreward.
As if it was life's greatest adventure.

How I wish I were so easily pleased.
That every step that I take,
no matter how simple would be
like a journey to wonderland,
not just another mile of stone and sand.

We need to learn to understand;
to see in every day something special
God has planned.

"Not that I complain of want, for I have learned in
whatever state I am, to be content." Philippians
4v11

STILL SMALL VOICE

"Who whispers on a narrow mountain path"?

I cannot hear properly, my mind has other
thoughts,
other more interesting ideas that begin
and end with me in full control.

Lord, your voice I expected to hear in thunderous
cacophony,
The loud and unforgettable performance
of a trained performer,
or in the earth-shaking destructivity of a warlord
in
the belligerent throes of conquest.
Maybe, in the lightning flash, spectacular electric
currents lighting up the skyline,
turning people's heads with its artistic splendour.
But who is this person speaking in a still small
voice?
He is patiently assured yet disturbingly calming in
influence.
Is it I who need to listen?
Is it I who need to concentrate or miss
the moment which passes quickly when You, my
Lord, speaks?
There was a hush and all who gathered around
Him listened intently to what he said, for the
words He spoke were Spirit and life and made

sense to their existence.
Make sense of my existence, Lord, that I may exist
for You; Lord, please calm the busy thoroughfare
of voices Fighting for control of my thoughts so
that I might hear You only
and in hearing You, hear others better.

'And there he to a cave, and lodged there; and
behold, the word of the Lord came to him, and he
said to him," What are you doing here, Elijah?"
"He spoke," I have been very jealous for the Lord,
the God of hosts; for the people of Israel have
forsaken the covenant, thrown down thy alters
and slain thy prophets with the sword; and I,
even I am left; and they seek my life to take it
away. "And he spoke, "Go, forth, and stand upon
the mount before the lord!" And behold the Lord
passed by, and a great and strong wind rent the
mountain, and broke in pieces the rocks before the
Lord, but the Lord was not in the wind; and after
the wind, an earthquake, but the Lord was not in
the earthquake; and after the earthquake a fire,
but the Lord was not in the fire; and after the fire
a small still voice. And when Elijah heard it, he
wrapped his face in his mantle and went out and
stood at the entrance of a cave. And behold, there
came a voice to him, and said,
"What are you doing here, Elijah?" 1 Kings 9-13

DIFFERENT

We're different
and sometimes I let
that difference
come between us.

May Jesus' love
better
draw us together.

'And Jonathon, Saul's son, arose and went to David
at Horesh, and encouraged him in God' 1 Samuel
23v16,

LIGHT

"Who stands at the door and knocks?"
I am the man who has come to an end;
an end of all struggle and strife,
high ideals, ambition and planning.

There is so much that I have not experienced of
life,
so much that I do not know; only the reality
that you open the door when someone knocks,
and the certainty that it is right to do so.

When I opened the door to you, Lord
I was a vessel emptied of the knowledge that I
knew the way.
Lost as I was in my sin, I was lost for the words to
say.
Lost to a world bent on destruction and vice,
breaking all promises and set in its lies.

I opened the door to let the light in.
It revealed me in poverty, locked in my sin.
You unlocked my door, releasing your love to heal
me within.
Now I am unburdened, unashamed and in need of
loving.

'The Lord is God, and he has given us light' Psalm
118v27

LET NOT YOUR HEART GROW WEARY

Let not your heart grow weary,
let not your love grow cold.
For it is I, your Lord, who love you and leads you.
Let not your love grow cold.

For I, Your Lord, am the strength of your life.
Let not your love grow cold.
For in Me you have life abundantly;
to me you are more precious than gold.

Cast off your fears for the future;
cares for the days of your life.
Take up my cross, follow me each day;
therein is death to all strife.

Put on my garment of mercy;
my garments of praise and of love,
then you will neither be cold or weary;
your heart will be full of my love.

'Put on then, as Gods chosen ones, holy and
beloved,
 compassion, kindness, lowliness, meekness and
patience. And above all these things put on love.'
Colossians 3v12

BIRD SONG

Have you tried
chaining down a song
that won't be held,
Whose melody uncaptured
holds a freedom note?

Or have you heard
how a bird when it sings
is not ashamed for its
song to be heard
but sings clearly into the wind
and holds humanity enchanted
with the beauty of its song?

HEART'S RELEASE

My stream has dried up
the source is blocked by stones and leaves
in the forest below rocky peaks
there is water enough when the rains come
to flood my stagnant soul with peace
and break the dam of this uncertainty--

One day I hope this hurt I feel will cease;
Until then may the stream run
in my waking dream and bring hearts release.

YOU CANNOT SEE THE WIND

Can you see the wind as it blows

through a grove of trees?
Only the leaves as they fall to the earth
and blow away.

I cannot see you, Holy Spirit

as you blow through my trees of pride;
only see the leaves of self will fall to the earth
and die.

I can feel a change of heart, having ceased its
labour,
blossom under Gods love and favour.

'The wind blows where it wills, and you hear the
sound of it, but you do not know whence it comes
or whither it goes; for it is with everyone who is
born of the Spirit' John 3v8

SMALL IS BEAUTIFUL

I expect too much
but see not the minute flower,
the daisy and the eglantine,
so small, yet with such power
to melt the heart of man!

'Also in this He shewed me a little thing, the
quantity of an hazel-nut, in the palm of my hand;
and it was as round as a ball. I looked thereupon
with eye of my understanding, and thought:
What may this be? And it was answered generally
thus; it is all that is made. I marvelled how it
might last, for me thought it might suddenly have
fallen to naught for littleness. And I answered in
my understanding; it lasteth, and ever shall last
for that God loveth it. And so All-thing hath the
Being in the love of God. In this Little Thing I saw
three properties. The first is that God made it, the
second is that God loveth it, and the third, that
God keepeth it. But what is to me verily the Maker,
the Keeper, and the Lover, - I cannot tell; for till I
am substantially one'd to Him, I may never have
full rest nor very bliss; that is to say, till I be so
fastened to Him, that there is right nought that
is made betwixt my God and me. Dame Julian of
Norwich Revelation of Divine Love

THE THOUGHT FLOWER

The thought behind your present held me
even in my deepest pain as I held onto
a ledge over a precipice of suffering one
cannot quite name and doubted my own sanity.
Each time I claimed Jesus's name, yet each time a web
held me tighter until I was enmeshed in my own blame.

I looked at the flower; it was your consoling face.
You smiled and spread your petals and I even
heard you call my name.
"Philip, Jesus suffers the same."

A thought, that grew into a comfort and settled
there beneath my breast.
If not for the consolation of your voice; the
softness of your heart;
the thoughtful tenderness of your interest, when
you said,
"Philip, abide in His strength."

And at length I did-
So am content.

"For Christ also suffered once for sins, the just for
the unjust, that He might bring us to God ..." 1
Peter 3v18

AUTISTIC MASKING

I have always looked upon myself as a loner,
someone who does not fit in to normal society.
Someone who goes out of his way to dwell in
the background. It is so easy for me to shun the
limelight; to hover in the shadows away from
earthly glares. Yet at certain times I have sought
to be accepted and masked my feelings in such a
way that I became an actor on a stage; playing my
part for all I was worth. It is only recently that
I have accepted I am autistic. ASP or Asperger's
Syndrome to give it its full title. As a child I hid
in fantasy, unaware of any condition other than
my shyness and unbearable fear. At time I used to
cry out in the night. Even at times my condition
became unbearable. My dreams became a place of
sanctuary; also, time on my own spent on a hilltop
and in the sublime countryside away from the
hubbub of noises and the bustle of human activity
acted like meditation to calm my spirit and
helped to keep me whole. I certainly was no team
player. In fact, I hid who I really was and probably
accepted I would spend my life alone. I suppose
in some ways my writing became a screen which
I hid behind. I am sure I am not alone. When I
created my poetry website, I found hundreds
of people like me. I was not alone anymore and
revelled in the constant stream of shared thoughts

that engulfed me like a tide. My biggest salvation was being blessed with a wonderful wife who became my soulmate, and accepted me for who I was and through her love helped to create a new person from the old.

NATURE'S SWEET ELATION

A morning like today
sees me rising from my bed,
catching the first suns ray,
birds sing a sweet refrain
calling to the wild within,
healing all my hurt and pain.

I have a song to sing this morn
in thanks to God for all creation.
I'm glad that I was born
to feel natures sweet elation.

RENEWAL

I am pressed into this world's mould.
Into a way of thinking that conforms to a set pattern.
I think sometimes that my thinking ought to
take on a more purposeful nature;
a nature with a divine seal of approval.
If the hills are to be my terrain, I must travel light
to reach the summit of His designs.

Above the clouds the pressure eases
and I am walking close to God.
He bears my burden on the slopes
and my thinking is transformed.
In His glory I rise against the flow of pressure;
overcoming by His blood.

'Do not be conformed to this world but be transformed by the renewal of your mind, that you may prove what is the will of God, what is good and acceptable and perfect' Romans 12v2

GIVING OURSELVES

I grow it in a garden though I did not see it grow,
before I knew you my world was full of weeds,
there was no room for your fruit of love to grow.
But you took me by the hand and planted me in
your garden. There are still weeds but by your love
they will not thrive and fill again the ground that
you have hoed.
You trust me Lord to keep your garden free from
weeds that flower and sow.
So, in your garden I grow free to bear the fruit you
require of me; and as you send down showers of
blessings my love for you will never lessen but
increase and grow.
As joy brings strength to weary limbs and love
being
the fruit of suffering through weather perverse
and stormy yet will I not hold my fruit to me but
share your fruit of love abundantly.
Sharing with others who need to know the grace
of God to help them grow, and need someone who
cares enough to show that love to them by giving
themselves as an offering!
"They shall come and sing aloud on the height of
Zion, and they shall be radiant over the   goodness
of the Lord, over the grain, the wine, and the oil,
and over the young of the flock and the herd; their
life shall be like a watered garden, and they shall

languish no more."   Jeremiah 31v12
ESV

TWO LOVERS HIDDEN IN GOD

We, two lovers find security
in one another's arms.
Are held as first precious fruit,
safely in our Masters hands,
and we will never come this way again.

The future spans, for us, an uncharted sea.
Yet, our lives are hidden with Christ in God
and will forever be.
Our hope is hidden with Christ in God.
He has set His seal upon our love,
and will feed it as a mother feeds her child,
unselfishly.

OVERCOMING

They shade my world,
these overhangs of unproductive gloom.
The sun through chinks of light
attempts to reveal my room,

The room where I always come
when trouble shows its ugly head.
At times like this I sulk and brood
and wish that I were dead.

Even shadows cast their own shadows,
and beneath this canopy, so mean,
I sweat out all remorse and fears
for what might have been.

Yet through the gloom my spirit looms
as a knight with sword in hand,
wrestles to combat the gloom
and with his help to stand.

Chinks of light fall over me,
they cast out all my fears.
My knight has overcome the foe
and in my heart new hope appears.

COMMITMENT

As I walk with you
our needs are met,
the road less rugged;
no need to fret.

As I talk with you
all self-thoughts flee.
My eyes fresh set
on only Thee.

THE STRICKEN DEER BY WILLIAM COWPER

I was a stricken deer, that left the herd
Long since; with many an arrow deep infixt
My panting side was charg'd, when I withdrew
To seek a tranquil death in distant shades.
There was I found by one who had himself
Been hurt by the archer. In his side he bore,
And in his hands and feet, the cruel scars.
With gentle force soliciting the darts,
He drew them forth, and heal'd, and bade me live.
Since then, with few associates, in remote
And silent woods I wander, far from those
My former partners of the peopled scene;
With few associates; and not wishing more.

PRIVATE SOLDIER J.J.W KILLED IN THE FIRST WORLD WAR 1917

Someone found this poem in a church
near the battlefields

"With a Friend"

Look, God, I have never spoken to You,

but now I want to say "How do You do?"

You see, God, they told me You didn't exist,

And, like a fool, I believed all this'

Last night from a shell hole I saw your sky
And figured then they had told me a lie.
Had I taken time to see things You made
I'd have known they weren't calling a spade a
spade.

I wonder, God, if You'd shake my hand.
Somehow, I feel You will understand.
Funny I had to come to this hellish place
Before I had time to see Your face.

Well, I guess there isn't much more to say,
But I'm sure glad, God, that I met You today.
I guess the zero hour will soon be here,
But I'm not afraid since I know You're near.

There's the signal-I've got to go.

I like You lots, I want You to know...
Look now, this will be a horrible fight,
Who knows? I may come to Your House
tonight.

Though I wasn't friendly to You before,
I wonder, God, if You'd wait at Your door?
Look, I'm crying-me! -shedding tears!
I wish I had known You these many years.

Well, I have to go now, God, goodbye....
Strange, since I met You, I'm not afraid to die.

SEE THINGS DIFFERENTLY

Lord,
give her the wings to fly
up into the blue and peaceful sky
so, looking down she may see
things differently.

'God lifted us up from the grave into glory along
with Christ, where we sit with him in heavenly
realms-all because of what Christ Jesus did'
Ephesians 2v6TLB

LISTENING

Rest so transient, the current of life runs fast and
deep,
pressures force out time, no time left to think and
speak.
Yet, peace is not only found in solitude but in the
busiest street;
a place where noise encroaches and commerce
speaks loudest.
Even there can be a perfect rest for all who trust
God
and with whom that trust is fully blessed.

Jesus, let my mind be tunes as an instrument to
your particular theme
that we might know just when you speak my Lord;
our every breathing moment a listening.

'The righteous flourish like the palm tree, and
grow like a cedar in Lebanon. They are planted in
the house of the Lord, they flourish in the courts
of our God. They still bring forth fruit in old age,
they are ever full of sap and green, to show that
the Lord is upright; he is my rock' Psalm 92v12-15

"This is my simple religion. There is no need for
temples,
   no need for complicated philosophy, our
own brain, our own heart is our temple. The

philosophy is kindness." Dalai Lama

PANTHEISM

1/ a doctrine which identifies God with the universe, or regards the universe as a manifestation of God.
2/ the worship or tolerance of many gods.

"I believe in the cosmos. All of us are linked to the cosmos. So, nature is my god. To me, nature is sacred. Trees are my temples and forests are my cathedrals. Being at one with nature." Mikhail Gorbachev

"Everything is interwoven, and the web is holy." Marcus Aurelius

PATTERNS IN THE SKY

To look into the sky at night,
star patterns emblazoned on my mortal sight;
myriads of beauteous creatures I see
and even more rest upon farther shore:
Far beyond a sparkling milky sea.

> Each diurnal sparkling light
> pierces my short-lived mortal sight;
> tinker with my flimsy brain so in
> my mind I hear the sweet refrain of
a goddesses singing voice calling me to journey
upon a sea of stars for an eternity of warm
intensity,
in the pleasure of her cosmic arms.

> The day comes when my spirit
> must leave these body shackles
> far behind, follow after the divine
> across milky sea and gulf of years
> that separates me from all my fears:
> Healing my conscious burdened
mind.

What treasure will I find amongst
the Stars that wildly glisten in my mind?

> Through countless constellations

I will find the daughter of the night,
shining bright in marriage lace of

stars

glistening in the cosmos of her eyes;
beckoning for me to enter in
among her swirling diadems
that seethes with spectral intensity;
tearing lose my disguise:
Desire burning, burning as stars.

A man looks up into the skies,
sees a lady of the night, stars glistening bright,
wrapped in the shining circling arms of her lover's
charms.

SET FREE

Do you see that bird in flight,
so gracefully it flies into sight upon a wild wind?
Is it not a beautiful fragile thing?

Small, yet powerful enough to touch my heart
as mere human words cannot.
With the bird my soul is lifted into the air:

I am more peaceful there.

Excerpt The Great Hymn of Aten by Akhenaten Pharaoh of Egypt.

Thou appearest beautifully on the horizon of
heaven,
Thou living Aton, the beginning of life!
When thou art risen on the eastern horizon,
Thou hast filled every land with thy beauty.
Thou art gracious, great, glistening, and high over
every land;
Thy rays encompass the lands to the limit of all
that thou hast made:
As thou art Re, thou reachest to the end of them;
(Thou) subduest them (for) thy beloved son.
Though thou art far away, thy rays are on earth;
Though thou art in their faces, no one knows thy
going.

DESIRE

I am fed umbilical within a watery sphere,
waiting to be born and when my time has come
I am coaxed through finite space, moving out of
necessity,
through a birth canal into the light of existence.
My mother nurtures me with the milk of
kindness.
As a baby clings to her mother's teat for
sustenance
so, you suckle me with the nectar of paradise.
Statuesque is my mother's beauty.
As a goddess she sits regally upon her raffia
throne.
Her breasts like Mount Olympus from which flows
Ambrosia;
as did Hera who nurtured a young Hercules-
He of the strength of bulls and roar of lions.

Mother; from such as this your galaxies were
formed.
Gala, which in Greek means milk!
Such is expansion of stars that swirl
into patterns of animals and birds.
Unconquerable heroes of myth and legends,
from a single particle they expand to infinity,
beginning as a twinkle in your eye.
Such extra-terrestrial ideas are consummated

through loves expression that burns as fire
within this sweltering furnace of the heart.
Ideas that coalesce and exist to procreate.
I exist as part of constellations.
My male organ swells to meet your need.
To nurture new life in a womb, touch
unblemished skin.
You find fulfilment in nurturing another Hercules
or a Diana.

One day I will wander in the beauty of Elysium
Fields.
One day I will be joined with the elements that
once
harboured life but now are dormant and still
until awakened to make a final journey among the
stars;
becoming immortal in a dazzling moment when I
am set free
in the swelling soup of realization.
I look at you tonight and see within the
constellations of your eyes
other restless universes forming from poignant
memories of desire.

SANDS OF TIME

How fast can the sands of time run?
You grasp every second until it's gone
rolling and sweating every moment.
From spring to winter life imitates
birth and eventually dying.
Each and every colour that I see;
every rainbow that appears as
an arc in the vastness of eternity.
How fast can the sands of time run?
You grasp every second until it's gone
zooming as a car down a faded highway,
gathering speed as the journey goes
breathlessly panting all the way.
Time leaves carcasses that
animal's one-day will feed upon.

How fast can the sands of time run?
You grasp every second until it's gone.
You put on your trainers and you run
down the raggedy lane that winds
through heather and bracken on the heath,
over dunes that stretch limbs and expand lungs;
sweat beading over forehead like a waterfall onto
grainy sand. My precocious life travels inevitably
on and on
into a far distant future we all set our hopes upon.
Before me I can see a hopeful golden sun, an

endless blue sea.

VISION QUEST

Rising up inside my heart my shade embarks on
a journey of soul and I am becoming whole.
Becoming as one with the Moon and Sun,
with the earth beneath my feet:
I am where pathways meet.

The forest and the everglade,
the prairie and the desert too
have come into my view.
I see the power of all,
the subtle colours in the Fall;
the blazing white of mountain snow
become a part of all I know.

The grizzly in her glory;
the eagle in her high eerie;
the wolf with cubs in her lair,
all these tell a wondrous story
told with pure delight and care.
I place sticks carefully to build a fire
while Mother Nature burns a funeral pyre.

From coast to coast my journey goes,
envisioned by someone I used to know
yet held in the background in my mind
until he broke free to find his kind.

So, I pace the world in vision quest

hoping to find what the Gods have blest.
I will now leave to claim what is mine
in forests, deserts, mountains;
in moon chill and summer sunshine.

I fly the thermals in my mind
along the canyons of mankind,
through woodlands and valleys
and mountains high;

I breast the peaks into the sky
and looking down and see the rolling sea,
the gentle stream and river wide.

Of all these, water meant the most to me,
as salmon make their journey from the sea
to leave its spawn inside of me.

So, I will never stop my journey till I find
those gentle harbours in my mind.

LIVING AT THE END OF YOUR TETHER

(Another polar conquest)

Come, see the shadows in the snow.
The wild wind howls like a banshee.
Ghosts form, only to disperse.
We have many, many miles to go,
more torturous miles than one
can possibly comprehend.

A friend of us all has reached his furthest end.

We are comrades all, held together,
As we are, by the need to survive
struggling against these awful elements,
summoning the deepest and best
from our ailing inner resources.
Our comrade's unflinching assurances,
there when we really need them.

Another man within our mortal frame,
strengthened by such sterling companionship,
through blistering hardship,
becomes an eternal flame;
victorious in life's closing moments.
(In memory of Oats) Expedition to South Pole
1912

PAGAN THOUGHTS

"True, we love life, not because we are used to living, but because we are used to loving. There is always some madness in love, but there is also always some reason in madness." Friedrich Nietzsche

"I'll try a pagan friend today, thought I, since Christian kindness has proved but hollow courtesy." Herman Melville

METAMORPHOSIS

The storm broke, rain falling, nicking my skin like knife strokes. The deafening crash of thunder broke the eerie silence, turning the world upside down. Lightning struck clinically across the broad expanse of Boxhill, searing a lone regal oak of one of its branches, setting a valance of crows flapping and coring into a desperate sky. As the world turned so, I stood statue still out in the midst of the deluge, letting the incessant rain soak my ragtag clothes down to my pitiful skin.

Boxhill had been my refuge and strength. On balmy summer days I escaped from my humdrum existence in the valley, vaulted the dilapidated wooden stile, trudging across the muddy track until I arrived at the river's edge. This river, called Mole, held special memories gleaned from a happy childhood spent in fishing and play. All filed away in memories ample store to bring refreshment to my jaded present and collapsing future. Stepping stones breached the river; in days gone by I imagined I was a miniscule Robin Hood, staff held firmly in hand and just in case a catapult, pockets bulging with serrated stones.

Today the stepping stones looked different. The river flowed higher and with greater intensity from the incessant rainfall, lapping at the crest of the stones making them treacherous to the careless traveller. I had no choice but to push ahead across the river and my rising fear, risking a fall into the muddy torrent. Probably better for me if I just let myself fall, letting the river drag me down into the depth where my pointless existence can ignominiously end. Yet I still held onto some vestige of sense so I continued gingerly across the flood and arrived with wet feet and socks but little else on the far side where the wood began its journey upward to the hill's boundary.

Why was I in this desperate state of mind? My own fault I'm afraid. Putting all my resources and trust in shares that dissolve like the mist, taking my families money and my dignity with it. Too late now! Too late to make amends. In gentler times the wood held magical significance. The smell of spruce and pine stimulated my being. The call of a warbler and the scuffle of squirrels acted as balm

to my being. Now, damp and decidedly deflated the trees loomed over me like questioning fingers and seemed to wrap me in gloom. By will power alone I trudged onward, up the slippery slope, losing my grip at times on the way, having to hold onto slippery trunks that cut my hands, opening sores. Each step took me falteringly upwards until I arrived at the gorse and grassy slope upon my hillside.

What was I doing here? I don't know. I only knew that my choices were extinguished and that all hope had departed. Only on this hillside had I found contentment, a peace of mind that eluded me now. So, I found myself in the midst of a storm from without and within. Dark clouds rested over my mind, seeming to sap my brittle will. I opened my eyes to look over the world edge, down to the valley that had become my downfall. It was then I noticed among the grasses the butterflies. They had picked a place of shelter beneath an overhanging rock and their coloured wings filled me with a jolt of surprised longing. Suddenly, by some intuitive spark of conscious thought I saw the folly of my ways. It was like I had been cocooned in my own selfish chrysalis; my deluded thoughts had trapped me in self-pity and loathing.

The butterflies captured my attention and entranced me with their beauty, so fragile, yet, so beautiful with their gossamer wings. So short lived yet filling each moment with endearing charm and pleasure. I was suddenly lost in wonder and made a wish to a God above that I so desired to spread my wings and fly into a new and wondrous future unhindered by selfish desires and longings.

The sun broke through the clouds and the butterflies flew heavenward on the gossamer wings and I sat upon the grass in my soaking clothes, letting the sun dry me and heal my spirit within, soothing the hurt away.

'According to an American Indian Legend, if any one desires a wish to come true, they must first capture a butterfly and whisper that wish to it.

Since a butterfly can make no sound, the butterfly cannot reveal the wish to anyone but the Great Spirit who hears and sees all. In gratitude for giving the beautiful butterfly its freedom, the Great Spirit always grants the wish. So, according to legend, by making a wish and giving the butterfly its freedom, the wish will be taken to the heavens and granted.'

TIME

Time
overtakes, even
blocks good intentions,
hinders me catching up
moments.

DRIFT AWAY

I drift away
on the wind spray
that drives my raft
out to sea.

On mountain waves
that force their way
through pores that breath.

Alone am I,
sun scours my flesh
from off me,
tearing strips away
to fall inconsequentially
into the sea,
sinking deep
where crabs scuttle
along the sea floor,
clutching part of me
in their claws.

Sun, spray and rain
has torn my skin
and made me scared within
this shell of a body
that protects the home in me.

I drift in deadly currents

and with the wind's rages
I am sprung loose
from man-kinds cage
to be unravelled by forces
far stronger and stranger
than any man has made:

If I survive then let it be.

THE WOODLAND IN THE SPRING

The woodland glade is regaled in flowers.
Could it be a wedding bouquet from some higher power?
Fairy folk dance in rings to the song a Dryad sings.
He is as ancient as the earth and knows who gave him life and birth.

Who is it that comes alone to this woodland glade?
Who passes invisibly into its inner sanctuary?

It can only be the one whose spirit is forever young;
whose youth will never fade but live on in rain and sun.

I come in awe, holding no power humbled as I am this early hour.
Spring has at last given birth to crocuses that bedeck good Mother Earth.
The birds in the treetops sing of warm, light days to come.
My tired heart feels sweet contentment; my spirits warm.

MULTIVERSE

The path that I did not take and a life which I never
lived.

Time enshrouded in a grey mist.
People whose names I'd once known, forgotten
now.
Skin felt soft an age ago, ghostlike now.
Unreal, like an apparition, faded memory.
I begin to think that there are different
versions of me across the years.
So many paths seem to intersect.

Did I take the safe path out of necessity
or was it predestined by some higher power?
At times the forest appeared denser,
valley deeper or hill higher.
No steady slope or easy climb;
the sea almost always rough;
beach dunes clinging to tired limbs.

I'm afraid more than once I cried.

The lonely shadow always tried
so hard to reach the other side.

ASHES OF A BRAVE

Our warrior chief is but ashes in my hand;
ashes that mingle with the sand.

Our brave chief's body is burnt upon a funeral
pyre.
His days on earth have run its course.
Now he rides the ranges in the netherworld.
Maybe he rides on conquests new.
Maybe he flies with the eagles into the blue,
across ethereal canyons he flies unchained and
free
up through the mists into a boundless sky of
victory.

For him there are no boundaries anymore.
This is not at all like his past life
when he led his warrior band
across a stark and barren land.
Riding their pinto ponies stripped for war
against an oppressive conqueror whose
countless forces try to hem you in and
once you are caught will never let you out again.

Now our brave chief flies free
unhindered by the flesh that pulled
him down and always craved sustenance.
He now has joined his illustrious forefathers.
He has left us a scattered band of

tired warriors in a pitiful reservation;
with little food and no freedom anymore.

We are hemmed in on all sides by an enemy
who possess superior force of arms but lack the
code by which we live.
We shall never again in this world know the
freedom of the open range;
the charge of the buffalo and the flight of our
arrows.

The only hope left for us now lies
after the long shadows of our earthly death,
when we join our warrior chief who has found
peace at last and freedom to ride under blue and
endless skies.

If one listens attentively one can hear his war cry
calling us to follow him into a land where buffalo
cover the plains and where we can lay our burdens
down.

CAVE PAINTINGS

Cave paintings of chalky white
they circle my dreams tonight.
Faded pictures upon a cavern wall
in my consciousness I do recall,
travel forward to me through the vault of time,
creating images so sublime.
In my consciousness I see
myself painting what comes to me.
I'm dressed in bearskins for the cold
and wear a weathered look so very old.
My thoughts are excited as I draw
the quarry that we warriors saw.
At night we danced around the fire;
our trophy's we all admire.
The noble stag with horns of white
hang on my cave wall this very night.
All memories of so long ago
travel forward through time and I seem to know
that the feelings of my ancestor are the same;
we strive and work for earthly gain
and suffer all manner of stressful pain
as we hold onto what we own, group together
and cast our lots.

SHADOWS IN THE NIGHT

Etched upon my consciousness
a simple trick of mind's duress.
In the darkness of the night
spirits moved into my sight.
Visions of sinister harm,
striking with unerring charm,
unearthing fears I could not face,
moved my madness more apace.
A hole opened like a creature's jaw
and I was sucked into its gaping maw.
Projected as from a loaded gun,
I fell into a place that good men shun.

Falling, falling with little sense of time,
a prison sentence for my crime.
All fibre of my being held me enthral,
condemned me forever to fall.
Then a glorious light filled my gloom,
I awoke in my own room.
Now conscious of my mortal plight,
I shunned the torments of night,
laid hold of my immortal soul,
prised myself from that damned hole.

Since sunlight did awaken me,
I see the route of simplicity;
the taunts of a troubled mind
can harbour demons of a kind.

Rest assured I will not sleep;
I have an appointment to keep.

The sun has filled my tortured mind
now all fear has lifted and I find
that shadows cast upon a painted wall
can in the night make you fall.
Reflections in the corner of your eye
can burn away the heart of all desire.
It would please the Devil to intrude,
fit me for his evil brood,
but light obliterates fancies of the night
making my heart and mind alright.

WOODLAND GLADE

The woodland glade is filled with peace.
Sunlight streams through twig and leaf.
The mortal sees not, for he has not belief.
If he were to open his eyes, lose for a moment his disguise
then maybe he would see a glorious ceremony,

As across the glistening shallow brook
light footsteps trip softly with hardly a sound;
no sight that mortal man can see.
He has lost the sight he once had as a child,
is no longer content just to be.

If only he would open wide his eyes
then he would see the fairy folk,
gleefully laughing at their simple joke,
their clothing moving in a gentle breeze,
see faces in the bark of trees.

If he were to open his ear
he would hear haunting singing of a choir
that lifts his burden held so long.
Fear banished; courage given to persevere.

Likely as not, if he could truly know,
experience for himself the fairy glow
the future would show a face more benign;
with renewed hope, the sun would have to shine.

He looks at last with his heart and begins to see
glistening gold water rising from a fountain
around which fairy folk are dancing,
joyful in their play, enjoying every day.

Embrace the moment and he will find
beyond the realm of human kind
another wondrous world exists;
one that a child cannot possibly resist.

Likely as not you would have to choose
whether or not to stay or lose
what hold humanity had on you -
I would choose to dance with the fairies too.

DREAM-STATE

'Enter my dream with me.'

'Come deep into my sleep.
Become lost in memory.
See fleeting visions,
distorted reflections,
dim recollections.
Let me describe to you
fragments of sheer fantasy.'

'Enter my dream with me'
'Come sit by the fire and see
how visions transpire;
what music you can hear
as a ghostly figure draws near.'

'Come enter my dream and you will see
that which I most fear that moves
nearer and nearer to me.'

'Let the visions depart
for they trouble my heart.'
'I am lost in the dark!'

'Do not enter my dream with me!'

HINTERLAND

Crisp and bracing is the air as I trudge this
woodland trail on scuffed snowshoes. My
bludgeoned body protected from the scathing
cold by cloth in many layers. My mood changes
as my mind shudders at a blossoming anxiety
that creeps up on me as a footpad, taking control
of my senses, spearing me with irrational fear.
This woodland journey began innocently enough
as little more than an exercise in my manliness
yet now each step taken becomes more arduous.
Shadows form in the hinterland of my mind
taking on ill-omen characteristic that blot out my
reasoning.

Many centuries past these woods were home to
packs of wolves and feeding bears. At that time
the forest covered hundreds of miles yet this
very moment is being plundered and through
my imagination creating scenarios that do not
take into account time or distance. Am I merely
a pawn in another's game? Some creature is
invading the sanctity of a reasoning mind. When
had I last heard birds sing? Miles and miles back
down a track which had lost its footprints. Silence
pervades my ears and snowy whiteness assails the
retinas of my eyes. Every so often I seem to hear a
scraping yet cannot be sure of which direction it
comes. Each crack of twigs beneath my feet causes

a reaction making me to revert from a modern human animal to a Neolithic hunter gatherer. Instinct wraps me in furs as I trudge relentlessly into the hinterland of my own worst nightmares.

THE OLD MAN AND THE FAIRY

If a garden could speak it would tell you so many stories. In the formal cloths of the lawn and flower beds you would see the clearly the state of mind of the occupant of his estate. Some would see if they could peep for a moment into the back yard of a person's property the state of mind that vegetates in pity. The house and garden, in this tale, exists in the village of Humble Beginnings, in the lovely rural beauty of Devon, close to the moor land of heather and ponies of Dartmoor. In this idyllic setting 'Summer Cottage' abides, next to a glade of great age and mystery. Old Mr Green lives in this cottage, Thomas to his friends, if he had friends, which he does not anymore as he has become a recluse. It was twenty years before that his dearest Doreen died of cancer. She was the light of his life and the reason for his existence and almost immediately afterwards he succumbed to the sorry state that we now see him in today. He lost all his friends and became bitter and twisted like the brambles that smother his flowerbeds. Building a high brick wall around his ground and also his tormented heart he retreated in on himself and let himself go to seed.

Once he had been a happy man with everything to live for, a loving wife and many friends who he enjoyed a card game with and drank down a pint at the Swan and Goose, his local pub in the village. Now he is a shadow of his former self who sits wasting away upon his soiled garden chair in his overgrown weed infested garden which has run riot; such is also sadly the state of his besieged heart and mind. Thomas sits with a bottle of whisky, half-drunk already, the hour is still early yet he pours alcohol down his withered throat only stopping to cry, which he does frequently. His filthy hanky, wet with tears, his cloths stained with food from too many quick and easy meals from the local Co-op. His crying and deep vexation disturbs the tranquillity of this once peaceful setting, even over the high brick wall into the glade, the woodland that borders his particular kingdom. Small pointed ears twitch at the sound they hear. Small gossamer wings flutter and lift tiny ethereal bodies of two Fairies aloft to float like thistledown over the red brick wall to catch a glimpse of this human in so much distress. The Fairy folk live on an altogether different plain of existence from human beings. They live in the ether between worlds. They are magical and happy creatures whose existence is lost in the vault of time; they rely upon belief to exist. Once belief had been shared amongst other all creatures, human or otherwise, and they lived in harmony together. But that was long ago and now rational thought in these modern times had stolen the wonder that is Fairy. Yet in all of us there is a need to believe that outweighs our crusty logic and in those fleeting moments we catch a glimpse, even though for only a split second of the other side.

'He is tormented Thistle.' Laurel says in her soft voice as light as a tinkling bell.

'Yes, Laurel, he is passing through the veil of his tortured existence.' Thistle says, her voice sounding like a harp. 'Maybe we can help him find that spark of magic that he needs to exist?'

'Surely, we cannot interfere. It is not our place to interfere in the lives of human beings as we used to?' Laurel says, trying to bring some argument to the proceedings.

'His sorrow has breached the wall between our kingdom and his and is bringing despair for the first time for millenniums into our lives. Such grief he feels! It is destructive and has infected the very ground on which he sits.' Thistle trembles with this realization.

'Yes, we must try to resolve his troubled spirit else our lives will never be the same again.'

Laurel takes her wand from beneath her gossamer wings and also some fairy dust which she proceeds to empty upon Thomas's head; waving the wand she chants an incantation which Thistle also joins in singing. They sound to Thomas's ear like the murmur of the wind and the faint buzzing of bees on a plant. Thomas suddenly shakes and his eyes take on a startled look. Around him the garden is transforming; slowly at first. He rubs his eyes because he feels the drink has at last destroyed his brittle mind and he is beginning to see things. Yet as he looks again at the garden, he no longer sees long thistles, ragwort, bramble and long unkempt knee-high grass. As if by magic his garden is taking on the appearance of how it looked thirty long years before in much happier times, when life was rosy, well-kept and neat with flower beds, short grass and elegant statues and even a small vegetable patch.

Tom thinks he is dreaming, yet when he looks at his

hands they are no longer wrinkled and his nails no longer jagged and unkempt. What is even stranger he no longer smelt disgusting but clean and new like a young man, so thankful to be alive again. The homely smell of roast lamb, greens and potatoes on the boil wafts into the garden from the kitchen. Tom has such a feeling of unreality and he pinches himself hard and shudders for it hurt a lot. Yet still he cannot believe what his eyes, ears and nose are so obviously telling him. Then he has a thought that does not seem to come from his mind and he follows up this thought, almost believing for a moment that this thought may be true.

'Doreen.' Thomas calls out in a voice which is of a younger man. And through the open door of the kitchen elegantly walks his one true love. A smile regales her beautiful though mischievous face. Her blue eyes filled with the joy of life. Thomas stands up and immediately staggers, for his mind is finding it difficult to cope with the vision that he now beholds. Doreen's melodic sounding voice breaks through the muddle of his thoughts.

'Well dear, the dinner is almost ready and I did not want to disturb you as you looked so peaceful. You have been working so hard recently and deserve a good rest.'

'It's as though I have woken for the first time for years.' Thomas says, wiping his glasses with his now clean hanky to make sure that this is not an illusion. But of course, it is not an illusion but something much more magical than that. He then reaches out his arms and takes his Doreen into them, pulling her to his chest and kissing her on her radiant face, saying 'I love you darling, I will always love you, my treasure.'

'Today, does feel a special day' she says, giving him a kiss on his lips, 'a very special day. You could almost say we have been blessed.'

Laurel and Thistle flutter on gossamer wings in air currents between one existence and the next, the feeling calm descend upon their magical kingdom. The tide of darkness has been frustrated and dissipates into the bowels of the earth through the hollow of a gnarled and withered tree. Laughter can be heard; the tinkling music of the dancing fairy folk as they party in the grove of trees between worlds. If one listens carefully one can hear the laughter and happiness of two contented souls wrapped in one another's arms in a garden paradise that they will forever call home.

FAITH
The Golden Key - George Macdonald

Then the Old Man of the Earth stooped over the floor of the cave, raised a huge stone from it, and left it leaning. It disclosed a great hole,

"That is the way," he said.

"But there are no stairs!"

You must throw yourself in.

There is no other way.

WHERE TRANQUIL WATERS FLOW

Sometimes I just pass the time of day watching the tall ships as they are born along by the steady currents that make passage through the waters of this idyllic place possible. I allow myself to float upon steady currents and the balmy breezes. It would be wise to heed the waiting storm just over the horizon awaiting the unwary traveller. My boat has a glass bottom so I can see the skittering explosion of fish life as they attempt to escape the onslaught of a predator's feeding frenzy. I was born on this island; born to float and to swim these sultry waters and frothy waves. Born to walk barefoot upon torrid sands, over rocks and dip my hands into rocky pools touching urchins and peeler crabs; leaving a part of me free-falling through seaweed streamers and barnacle encrusted caves. So, I escape where no one else can follow, down into the mystic depths, where one's awareness is made more defined and where danger is but one mistake away. I must escape life's evil undertow. To grasp all that's well in life; to drift where tranquil waters flow.

METAPHYSICAL THOUGHTS

Curiosity is a wonderful gift and I love the power of thoughts. My thought processes are often complicated by my disability as my mind overthinks, yet with medication my mind is slowed down and thought processes contained. I digress! Metaphysics, as the dictionary definition says is the branch of philosophy that deals with the first principles of things, including abstract concepts such as being, knowing, identity, time and space: as a noun 'they would regard the question of the initial conditions for the universe as belonging to the realm of metaphysics or religion'

My thoughts on belief have changed over the years but I suppose I have hope in a personal God and would call myself Christian but am open to what other people in this world believes whether its other religions or evolutionary processes. What I get excited about is the wonders of nature and evolution. The universe is so vast and old that I must not limit my thoughts and so make it too small. Also because of the fragile nature of my mind I refuse anymore to get trapped in another person's delusions about the nature of God. Most of these faith poems came to birth over forty years ago and when I read them today, I feel glad that they came forth from my imagination in an act of creation to encourage and plant fresh hope to souls who need a lift in their lives from the doldrums of insecurity.

LOSS

Leaving the heart in mortal fear and can
bring upon itself, many cares.
Sorrow as a bird can try escaping into the air,
yet so easily be caged by grief.
Only love has the power to bring relief.
Freedom exists only in how much we care.

Gnosis? nausis)/noun - knowledge of spiritual
mysteries. Esoteric knowledge of spiritual truth-
held by the ancient Gnostics to be essential to
salvation. Gnosticism is the belief that human
beings contain a piece of God (the highest good
or a divine spark) within themselves, which has
fallen from the immaterial world into the bodies
of humans. All physical matter is subject to decay,
rotting and death. These bodies and the material
world, created by an inferior being, are therefore
evil. Trapped in the material world, but its status,
the pieces of God require knowledge (gnosis) to
inform them of their status. That knowledge must
come from outside the material world, and the
agent who brings it is the saviour or redeemer.
Gnostic Christians- In phylosophical thought,
logos (word) was the principle of rationality that
connected the highest god to the material world.

"In the beginning was the Word (logos), and the Word was with God, and the word was God. He was with God in the beginning. Through him all things were made; without nothing was made that has been made. In him was life, and that life was the light of men." John 1v1 NIV

The arms of the Lord

Love takes the initiative.

It is not slow to do good.

before it is asked it acts.

Its response is always pleasing.

It does not look for personal gain

but sacrifices itself for the sake of others.

God is love, we are the arms of the Lord

which His love moves unconditionally through.

ABOUT THE AUTHOR

Philip Carmen

My name is Philip Carmen and I live in Hampshire, England. My wife is Shirley. We have been married for 42 years. Our children are Katy and Debbie. Our grandchildren are Isabella, Owen,  Anabel and Lincoln. My interests are reading, writing, drawing, painting, music and films. We both love nature and walk often and visit gardens. In the twilight years of my life I have no regrets.

Printed in Great Britain
by Amazon